A Quest For The Jewish Jesus

✡

Roni Mechanic

A Quest for The Jewish Jesus

Copyright © 2020 Roni Mechanic

All rights reserved.
ISBN: 9781790847815

Imprint: Independently published:

Shalom Radio UK

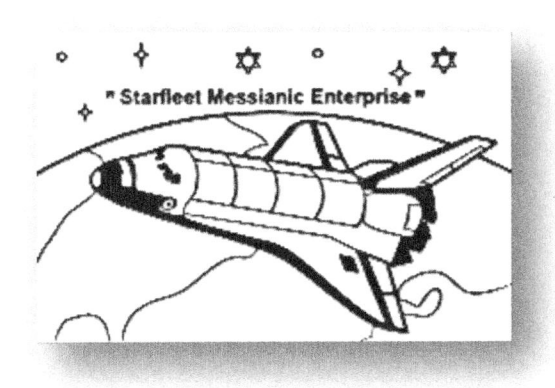

MTMI
Messianic Teaching Ministry International©
mtmi.teaching@gmail.com

DEDICATION

There are a number of people that I wish to dedicate this book to:

My beloved parents
Sonny (Thomas) and Anne Mechanic,
for their love and nurture in the Jewish faith of our fathers
*

Elisheva Mechanic my darling wife, life's companion and best friend
*

Peter Eliastam
who showed me the way of faith
"Psalm 32"

For dear R. – with love and prayer for you that you may be given the grace and strength to live for our God – as an "Israelite indeed in who there is no guile" – saved by the atoning blood of God's own sacrifice – His only begotten Son, our Messiah – ONE GOD, with the Father and the Holy Spirit.
"The Way, the Truth and the Life. "
*

Ecclesiastes 9:11 (KJV)
[11] "… the race is not to the swift, nor the battle to the strong,"
(An inscription in a copy of the Scriptures that Peter gave me)

Roni Mechanic

CONTENTS	PAGE
Chapter no. Description:	**no.**
I — Dedication	iii
II — Copyright Requirements	vii
III — Acknowledgments	viii
IV — Book Cover	ix
VI — Forward	1
V — Introduction	3
1 — My Background	5
2 — Personal Experiences of Anti-Semitism, and Anti-Judaism	11
3 — Prejudice: Anti-Zionism/Anti-Semitism: A new face of an old hate	17
4 — The Different Faces of Jesus	23
5 — The Aryan Jesus	29
6 — A Jewish View of Yeshua	37
7 — On Being Jewish	43
8 — Who is this Yeshua?	53
9 — In Search of the Jesus of History	61

CONTENTS	PAGE
Chapter no. **Description:**	**no.**
10 — In Paul's Defence	67
11 — The Human Response	75
12 — A Verbal Confession	91
13 — The New Testament	97
14 — "Has God Rejected His People?"	101
15 — Mahatma Gandhi Insufficient Atonement	105
16 — "I AM" of the Tetragrammaton	111
17 — The Place of Prayer	117
18 — My Personal Account	123
19 — The Power of the Gospel	131
20 — My Story	135
21 — On the 29th May 1969	141
22 — Don't Muddy the waters	147
23 — Self-identity	153
24 — Jews, God and Christian Renewal	159
25 — "Ambiguity, perplexity, & uncertainty"	163

Contents	PAGE
Chapter no. Description:	no.
26 — Jesus Freak	165
27 — Jewish and Christian Renewal	169
28 — Hebrew or Greek Bible?	175
29 — Apartheid South Africa: 1948 — 1994:	181
30 — Redeemer, Revealer, Judge and Creator	191
31 — Despair for a moment or a way of life?	195
32 — Modernity and Post-modernity	203
33 — The Holy Yehudi – Yeshua	207
34 — An Aliyah	213
35 — Last Words	219
36 — Bibliography	225
37 — Glossary of Terminology	232
38 — About the author	233
39 — End Notes	235

Copyright Requirements for Use of the Scriptures: ©

No Permission Required:
1. KJV - King James Version, Open domain, no copyright required.
2. THB - The Holy Bible, Translated from Ancient Eastern Manuscripts, Copyright © 1957 By A J Holman Company. Copyright has expired - no permission required.

Conditions of Use:
1. ESV - English Standard Version, "Scripture quotations are from The Holy Bible, English Standard Version (ESV), Copyright © 2001 by Crossway. Used by permission."
2. NIV - New International Version, "Scriptures taken from the HOLY BIBLE, NEW INTERNATIONAL VERSION, Copyright, ©1973, 1978, 1984 by The International Bible Society. Used by permission, Zondervan Publishing House. All rights reserved."
3. NRSV - New Revised Standard Version: "The Scripture quotations contained herein are from the New Revised Standard Version Bible. Copyright ©1989, by the Division of Christian Education of the National Churches of Christ in the USA. Used by permission. All rights reserved."
4. SEB - Stuttgarter Erklärungsbibel, Auflage 1992 © 1992 Deutsche Stuttgarter Erklärungsbibel, "Scriptures taken from SEB. All rights reserved."
5. TCJB - The Complete Jewish Bible: "Scripture quotations taken from the Complete Jewish Bible, Copyright © 1998 & 2016 by David H Stern. Used by permission. All rights reserved worldwide."
6. TOJB - The Orthodox Jewish Bible: "Scripture taken from the Orthodox Jewish Bible. Copyright © 2011, by AFI International. All rights reserved."

ACKNOWLEDGMENTS

Thank You:

A word of thanks to Dr Max Debono-De-Laurentis for his encouragement and suggestions in how to proceed with the writing of this book and general editing.

Also, thanks to Rev Stuart Harrison for painstakingly proof-reading my original book manuscript.

I did not learn theology in a vacuum, it is therefore with special thanks to a number of my theological educators who over the years have guided in my theological thought and development. Though there are too many to list here, nonetheless, without their help I would not have been able to write this book.

Without the editorial assistance of Donald Barker, a longstanding friend from South Africa, who now lives in Jerusalem, Israel, this manuscript would not have been edited to its high level of accuracy. Thank you.

In addition, a special word of thanks to my wife Elisheva Mechanic for her editorial suggestions and careful checking of the text before publication.

"A Quest for The Jewish Jesus"
*

Subtitle:
"Who do you say that I am?"
(Matthew 16:15)
Cover design by Roni Mechanic ©

A Quest for The Jewish Jesus

Genesis 22:8 KJV

And Abraham said, "My son, God will provide himself a lamb for a burnt offering": so, they went both of them together.

From a painting by Roni Mechanic©

A Quest for The Jewish Jesus

Forward

I recall some years ago while studying at Trinity Theological College in Bristol, UK, the librarian, as a way of introduction on the use of the college library, said, "There is no end of books" – (sounding more like *'boeks'* in his Northern Ireland, Ulster accent).

So why another book of theology and testimony? This is a good question – I feel compelled to share, not only my personal story, but also theological insights that I have gained in the nearly fifty years of walking along this long road that I have trod.

From my personal perspective, over these five decades I have worked in ministry, that includes inter-faith dialogue. I am also an artist, teacher, writer and internet blogger. In addition, I have travelled internationally, with some cross-cultural exposure in the *first world*, and the *majority two-thirds world* (the so called "third world"). I am widely read, with an interest in English literature, theology, missiology (science of mission), philosophy, psychology, sociology, history, art and politics. I have particularly focused on Jewish studies that includes Jewish-Christian relations and Holocaust studies. I hope that from my broad life experience I have something worthwhile to contribute to the wider debate about Jesus' identity as a Jewish first century luminary.

I invite you to join me on this journey of discovery in which, I will not only grapple with the issue of *'A Quest for the Jewish Jesus,'* but I will also look at many other facets that affect Jewish life and Jewish identity. You will meet the *Push-Me-Pull-You*[1] brigade along the way – some have attempted to pull Jesus this way and others pushed him that way!

Though Jews and Christians share a common heritage with both looking to Abraham as father, like Ishmael and Isaac and Jacob and Esau, very different paths have helped shape and forge the identities of two distinct people. Mutual mistrust; martyrdom, resulting in alienation, pain and sorrow; have helped separate them. Those Jews who seek to identify with Jesus often find themselves caught in the middle of two opposing forces. This can be a very challenging and uncomfortable place to be, yet it is possible to view it as a creative tension and not as something wholly irreconcilable and undesirable. The third mono-theistic faith of Islam is only briefly mentioned concerning the problems and opposition that both Jews and Moslems face concerning issues such as ritual slaughter and circumcision and the conflict over Israel-Palestine.

We should not forget that in both cases, Ishmael and Esau, as well as Isaac and Jacob, each had their own blessing from their earthly fathers which, in turn, were given by divine sanction. So too, Jews and Christians each have their own path that they follow within the divine scheme of things. A common destiny inextricably links these two faiths in a way that no other faiths do.

Not A Marginal Jew

All too often, those who oppose faith in Jesus as the Messiah of Israel have sought to, not only marginalise him, but equally those Jewish people who identify with him. However, it is my intention to show that to follow Jesus as Lord and Messiah, one is 'not a marginal Jew,' but one has become truly a completed and fulfilled Jew: An "Israelite indeed in whom there is no guile" (See John 1.47 - KJV).

Introduction

"Who do you say that I am" (Matthew 16:15)

Most Jewish and Christian scholars, agree that the historical Jesus of the first century was a Galilean Jew. His mother was Jewish, his Jewish followers called him "Rabbi," he spoke Aramaic, quoted the Hebrew Scripture in his teachings and he taught in the synagogue in Galilee and the Jewish Temple in ancient Jerusalem. His Hebrew name was Yeshua (God saves). Also, almost all his early followers were Jews. So how did we get from the Jewish Jesus of Nazareth of the first century of the common era to the Gentile Christian Jesus of today? Jewish people say, "look at what they have done to him – We don't recognise him at all - he does not appear to be a Jewish person."[2]

Yet, Rabbi Leo Baeck says, "He was a Jew among Jews; from no other people could a man like him have come forth and in no other people could a man like him work; in no other people could he have found the apostles who believed in him."[3]

A Quest for the Jewish Jesus

So, is it possible to discover the Jewish Jesus? This quest is not only something that is personally of great importance to me, but it also has a lot to do with the integrity of the of New Testament account of him; it also has to do with how Jewish people may approach him. Jewish and Christian scholars, in their quest for the historical Jesus, bring with them their own theological outlook and prejudices. We discover that the majority, rather than help resolve who Jesus is, serve to complicate the issues by further obscuring his true identity. While Jewish scholars have helped to reclaim him as a Jew, they universally deny that he is the divine Son of God and the Messiah. Moses Maimonides well illustrates this in his book *On Inter-faith Dialogue* when he said, "All these activities of Jesus the Christian, and the Ishmaelite (Muhammed) who came after him, are for the purpose of paving the way for the true King Messiah and preparing the entire world to worship God together…" Equally, many of the nineteenth and early twentieth century Liberal Protestant Christian scholars, while affirming his deity and messiahship, have all too often de-Judaized him. Equally, Catholic scholarship is vexed with a long history of anti-Judaism that has also obscured the Jewish heritage of Jesus, Mary and the early Apostles and disciples.

If he is not a Jew, then…

My quest for the Jewish Jesus, though related to "The Jesus Quest" of the nineteenth and twentieth century, follows a different line of enquiry and reasoning. I am not only concerned with discovering the Jesus of history, but more importantly, he must equally be the Jesus of faith. There can be no division between these dual aspects of his being. If he is not a Jew, and not the Jewish Messiah, then I can have nothing to do with him or the faith that he and subsequently his disciples proclaimed, because he would not be the Jesus who was anticipated and revealed in the Scriptures. This quest poses numerous challenges for the genuine enquirer. I have used the name Jesus and his Hebrew name Yeshua interchangeably. It is my sincere hope that you will discover the answer to the question posed by the subtitle of this book, "Who do you say that I am?"

A Quest for The Jewish Jesus

1 — My Background

I am of British Jewish parents who emigrated to South Africa in 1947, and I was born in Johannesburg in the second half of 1948. They were among the 688 British Jews that came to South Africa in 1947.[4] I was raised in a traditional English-speaking Jewish home. We regularly attended our local synagogue and I received Hebrew instruction in preparation for my Bar-mitzvah.

I recall my Torah portion: – Shabbat Shuva שבת שובה or "Sabbath [of] Return" – which refers to the Shabbat that occurs during the Ten Days of Repentance (Days of Awe), between Rosh Hashanah and Yom Kippur[5]. This Shabbat is named after the first word of the Haftorah (Hosea 14:2-10) and literally means "Return!" It is perhaps a play on shuvah, but not to be confused with Teshuvah – תשובה. This is the word for repentance. My journey to faith has been one of both return and repentance towards the God of Israel.
https://www.hebcal.com/holidays/shabbat-shuva

Formative Years

I was an active member of the Habonim (The Builders) Zionist Youth Movement (aligned to the Histadrut – Labour movement in Israel) – a secular Jewish Zionist organisation that not only encouraged Aliyah, immigration to Israel, but also included scouting and outdoor activities.

It was intellectually stimulating, but also tremendous fun. On the one hand, debates, discussions, Israeli cultural and political insights; on the other hand, camping, hiking and boating were just some of our activities. I was in the movement for ten years from the ages of 7 to 17 years old. I must express my gratitude to our very talented leadership, names like Simon Kuiper, Lee Flax, and David Gordon who were our group leaders, together with the Mendelsohn brothers (they became very important in Israeli Labour politics). Lee Flax introduced us to Franz Kafka, an existentialist writer and philosopher whose books, *Metamorphosis*, *The Trial* and *The Castle* had a significant influence on my young mind. I still personally consider Kafka's writing of importance and make reference to it in Chapter 31. We also considered the writing of Jean-Paul Sartre's books including *Nausea* and his book on *Anti-Semitism and the Jew*.

In my final year of high school in Johannesburg, South Africa, I became an active member of the debating society at Theodore Roosevelt High School, Roosevelt Park, Johannesburg. There were three subject that were off limits, namely, sex, politics and religion. As a consequence, we rebelled when a group of us established an informal forum that we called 'The Conversation Club' and our meetings took place off school property at friends' homes and our only agenda was sex, politics and religion.

Personally, there was an important link between the Conversation Club of students from Roosevelt High, and the influence of Habonim that included four of our members who were also involved in the Zionist youth movement as well as our local synagogue. We were young free-thinking liberals. I recall that we regularly invited guest speakers who were experts in their subject – a Jehovah's Witness, a Moslem, a left-wing trade unionist and a gynaecologist were just some of those whose ideas were considered. Discussions about sex, politics and religion helped to broaden our outlook and not to stay confined to the political and social conservatism that good South African girls and boys were expected to adhere to. These endeavours contributed to our intellectual development and helped me to also question my own religious and spiritual thinking. At one level, I found my Jewish faith fulfilling. However, at another level, I had a growing sense of a spiritual void in my life. This is sometimes referred to as 'a God-shaped hole or void.'

When the Rolling Stones said, "I can't get no satisfaction," they hit the nail on the head. Keith Richards and Mick Jagger expressed the places we often seek satisfaction – sex, drugs, rock 'n roll and consumerism fail to satisfy the longing in the human soul. We try to satisfy our appetites for creature comforts, and yet we still feel unsatisfied.

I recall asking two deep existential questions:

Where do we come from? Where are we going? These lie at the heart of humankind's quest for meaning that goes beyond the bounds of our material existence.

In this book I include autobiographically significant aspects of my journey to faith and beyond. Yet, I do not necessarily follow a chronological sequence. In addition to my quest for discovering the Jewish Jesus, I am also concerned about laying out the case for how Jewish people may encounter him as Yeshua of Nazareth. The personal anecdotes that I include will hopefully contribute to the overall theme. I also explore how a Jewish person who believes in Yeshua is able to not only maintain a Jewish identity, but also give expression to their faith within both the Jewish and Christian world.

In addition, the question of Jews living in a hostile world is something that impacted upon me personally from an early age. I discovered being Jewish placed an additional burden upon me. I experienced the phenomenon of anti-Semitism at a comparatively early age with my first encounter at primary school. I will say more about this in due course. My experience as a Jew is by no means unique for many of diverse backgrounds encounter xenophobia and race hatred early in their existence.

On my quest for the Jewish Jesus

It has been my desire for some time to lay out my faith journey. An equal concern is how Jewish people may reclaim Yeshua as their own. This is not just of academic interest to me, but it has a very personal significance because, as a Messianic Jew, one is caught in a world between the two faiths that sometimes feels a bit like someone trapped in "no-man's-land." This is a paradoxical position to find oneself in. I did not embrace Yeshua because I wanted to escape being Jewish, but as a consequence of my quest for life's meaning.

Fellow Jews say, "you are no longer Jewish," while many Christians say, "you are one of us now!" This is sometimes said in an almost triumphalist way, as if to say, "We have saved one more lost Jew!" This is both patronizing and hurtful. I was neither fleeing my Jewishness, nor was I seeking assimilation into the wider Gentile Christian society in which I found myself. I am proud of my Jewish heritage and upbringing. I have never stopped enjoying the rich Jewish life-experience which I claim as my own. My reason for embracing belief in Yeshua is a complex one.

Religious life is a very personal thing. Yet one must face numerous challenges in the desire to give expression to one's new faith as a Messianic Jewish. Also, there are questions that arise about one's identity. Can one attend synagogue (Orthodox), or temple (Reform) as well as church? Should one only eat kosher food and observe the sabbath and what other aspects of being Jewish should one keep? Does the Torah still have significance? When a Jewish person regularly attends a church service will it not, to all outward appearances, cause one to be identified not as a Jew but a Gentile Christian? Should one get baptised? This issue is viewed by the Jewish world as the cross over point. A Messianic Jewish identity offers a different paradigm to give expression to one's faith in Yeshua: Christian Jews; Jewish Christian; Hebrew Christian or Messianic Jew. Which one best describes the person you are?

Self-identity

Theological, sociological and psychological issues about personal identity need to be faced. Who are you? Where do you come from? Where are you going and how do you want to be identified? These are just some of the questions to ponder. These and other issues related to my own personal story are intricately woven into the warp and woof of its very fabric.

Theological issues surrounding personal identity help to address the question of how, according to Holy Scripture, we are viewed by God? This is a very important question and it helps to introduce an objectivity outside of ourselves. This adds a frame of reference beyond our narrow group and self-perception.

Roni Mechanic

The sociological implications of becoming a Messianic believer, for someone from a Jewish background, will have profound implications due to the hostility that the majority of Jewish people have towards Messianic Jews who embrace Yeshua as Messiah and Lord. Misunderstanding about what you will call yourself also characterises part of the question about identity that you will have to contend with.

We must not underestimate the psychological impact that we may encounter from those who show hostility. While there may be an emotional struggle at first, I must personally say that my decision to follow Yeshua has given me a sense of determination. I discovered an inner strength that enabled me to overcome any hostility and rejection that I faced. The personal conflict that I am confronted with is far outweighed by a sense of well-being and Godly contentment. This sense of wholeness transcends any human suffering caused by rejection. This is due to the indwelling *Ruach HaKodesh* (Holy Spirit), that the Scriptures call the Spirit; the 'Counsellor, Comforter, Guide, Go-between-God, Helper'. Though there is a personal cost to pay for becoming a Messianic Jew, the benefits far outweigh any negative issues that you may experience (see John 14.26). The concept of the activity of the Holy Spirit is not foreign to Judaism, for the work of the Spirit of God is ever present in the lives of the people of Israel. Judges, kings, prophets, prophetesses and priests alike were moved by the prompting of the *Ruach HaKodesh* (Holy Spirit) to perform and fulfil the work of God. This was not only for the benefit of Israel, but for the other nations as well. When the great outpouring of the Holy Spirit happened on the day of Pentecost, the limited work of the Spirit was then extended to all who yielded their lives to God through his Son Yeshua.

2 — Personal experiences of anti-Semitism, anti-Judaism and anti-Zionism

When at Franklin D. Roosevelt Primary School, Roosevelt Park, Johannesburg at the age of nine or ten years old, a fellow pupil from a Czechoslovakian background verbally abused me for being Jewish. Subsequently, this incident has caused me to ponder as to whether his father was a fascist who had collaborated with the Nazis during the Holocaust and then found his way to South Africa after the war? While this is conjecture on my part, having studied about the way that many Europeans under Nazi occupation collaborated with them during WWII, there is a reasonable possibility that his father could have been an active collaborator. What is clear, is that he harboured an anti-Semitic attitude and brought this with him to his new life in South Africa, influencing his son to be negative towards Jews.

"Hate speech" and physical assault

This incident was deeply distressing, and when I came home, I related it to my mother. She told me that during WWII in England, while doing war work in an ammunition's factory, one of the supervisors had verbally abused her for being Jewish saying, "You Jews need to go back to Palestine, because you don't belong here!" She discovered that he was a member of the Blackshirts who were fascists and members of the British Union of Fascists were who held a pro-Nazi outlook and who actively practised anti-Semitism.

In addition, my maternal grandfather Isaac had been blinded in one eye when a brick was thrown at him during the fascist unrest in the East-End of London during the 1930's, with him sustaining a detached retina. That was the side of his body that was struck by the bus that killed him during the blackouts during WWII. Therefore, I can hold the fascists indirectly responsible for his death.

Similarly, my father Thomas and his cousin Cyril lived and grew up in Birmingham. Their journey to school took them through an area of the city where anti-Semitic attacks regularly took place during the 1930's. My grandfather Hyman fashioned a whip for my father to use to fend off attacks from boys inspired by fascists to harass Jews. This begs the question as to whether Jewish people are safe anywhere? The phenomenon of anti-Semitism appears to be a universal problem.

Christian Anti-Judaism

I recall that while living in the Cape, South Africa, I was invited to share a word of testimony at an Afrikaans Reformed Church in the Cape Peninsula. The minister preached from a passage in the Gospels in which Jesus and the Pharisees locked swords. During his sermon he ranted against the Pharisees.

After his sermon, he invited me to come to the front and share a word of testimony of how I had come to faith. I felt insulted by his negative attitude. Had the minister deliberately preached that sermon for my benefit or was that part of his normal preaching? Whatever his motive, his theology was an appalling travesty and caricature of Judaism and if not deliberately anti-Semitic, it certainly reeked of anti-Judaism of the worst kind. It appeared that he had no understanding of the meaning and deep significance of what

I had experienced as a Jew who has come to faith in Yeshua. Neither did he show any empathy or insight into what a Jewish person faces in their sense of self-identity. He had missed the fact that many Pharisees became followers of Yeshua. The inheritor of the Pharisaic tradition is Rabbinic Judaism. Certainly, it has failures, but equally it also has great strengths and laid the foundation of Judaism.

The attitude of this minister of the Christian Reformed Church is not an isolated phenomenon but is symptomatic of a deeper malady within Christian theology and its outlook towards Judaism. This problem will be more fully explored and addressed in my journey of faith. Negative as well as positive influences help to shape what we believe. My response is always to look beyond the particular experience, whether good or bad, and ask the question as to why someone holds a particular viewpoint or attitude and not to simply reject out of hand what they represent.

Anti-Zionism

Anti-Zionism, while not directly linked to the question of whether God has rejected the Jewish people [Israel], helps to contribute to an antipathy towards Jews, Judaism and Israel. Anti-Zionism is increasingly having a negative impact upon the Evangelical Christian church. I have personally encountered this phenomenon when people discover that I am a Messianic Jew, and also someone who declares his love for Israel. I have been accused of being a 'Christian Zionist' (as if that is a crime), and of holding racist attitudes because I stand for Israel's sovereign right to exist as a nation. Many wrongly think that, if you support Israel, then you must be anti-Palestinian or anti-Arab. This accusation cannot be further from the truth. I have a number of Arab and

Roni Mechanic

Palestinian friends and I continue to seek ways to foster understanding and love between these two peoples whose destiny is inter-linked. (Visit my blog: www.hotrodronisblog.com).

Five Broken Cameras is an anti-Israeli propaganda film that was shot over a 5-year period, 2005-2009, by Palestinian Emad Burnat. It records the protests against the construction of a security barrier through the West Bank village of Bil'in. Burnat uses the destruction of his five cameras as a motif and connects the narrative to the development of his growing family. The film constructs a story that portrays the Palestinians as innocent, childlike victims fighting for land that has purportedly been stolen from them. Israelis are portrayed as cold-faced, heartless brutes. The Israelis are presented as acting only to cause suffering to the residents of Bil'in. This kind of one-sided accusation is becoming more frequent from Christians who follow the media and its constant negative reporting of Israel. The majority of these Christians have little, if any, first-hand contact with Israel or Israelis. They base their assertions on what they glean from an often-biased media.

What is the reason for Israel erecting the security barrier which is often referred to as the "apartheid wall?" It was built not to exclude Palestinians from Israel, but to protect its citizens from regular terrorist attacks. People conveniently choose to forget the deadly attacks that were a regular occurrence inside Israel. With the building of the barrier there has been a drastic decline of such attacks. In addition, there is another aspect of the conflict that is hardly ever reported by the mainstream media: "Rioters hurl rocks, Molotov cocktails and burning tires at the defence force and the security fence … Since the beginning of 2008, about 170 members of the defence force have been injured in these villages."[6]

A new face of anti-Semitism

Julie Burchill in *The Sunday Telegraph*, Sunday 3 February, 2019 (p 18), discusses a report by the Institute for Jewish Policy Research into the link between anti-Zionism and anti-Semitism, concluding that those who are active in attacking Israel are more likely than not to be anti-Semitic. She has considered why the hard left in British politics is inherently anti-Semitic. Some claim to be anti-racist on the one hand, yet on the other hand happily believe "that the Jews asked for it." Burchill calls this trend "Fresh 'N' Funky Anti-Semitism." Alas, this type of jumbled thinking and activism is dangerous. When Jewish politicians challenge their colleagues in the British Labour Party about their anti-Semitic attitudes, instead of being taken seriously they are accused of overreacting. The victim is blamed for the actions of the victimiser. This is both perverse and a sign of a great sickness within the body politic. It is like blaming the actions of the Nazis upon their victims. "Jews had it coming to them!"

Labour movement in Britain

Historically, the Labour movement in Britain was the natural home of many British Jews, with the Israeli Labour Party closely aligned to her sister movement in the UK. However, this is not the case anymore. British Jews are increasingly feeling insecure about their place in the Labour party and its future in Britain. This change has taken place due to the rise of anti-Semitism that has manifested itself within the Labour party. This is driven by those on the hard-left whose anti-

Roni Mechanic

Zionism has led to increased anti-Semitic attitudes being expressed towards Jewish Labour MP's. These attacks include hate-speech, hate-mail and death threats. "Debates over alleged antisemitism in the Labour Party may have sparked an increase in hate incidents against Jews in the UK, a report has found. The Community Security Trust (CST) recorded a record high of 1,652 incidents in 2018, an increase of 16 per cent on the previous year." Alas, many of the front bench Labour leadership have been slow in tackling the problems of anti-Semitism within the party.[7]

This trend that British Labour is manifesting is of personal significance to me due to my background in the Habonim movement with its close alignment to the Histadrut – the Labour movement in Israel (see p 5). As someone whose political inclination is of the centre-left, the hard-left's anti-Semitic shift of British Labour's current leadership is a source of deep concern. Together with many other fellow British Jews what is taking place at this present time within the Labour movement, is causing a deep sense of disquiet. Historically anti-Semitism found its home only in fringe hard-right fascist movements. However, with the UK's main opposition party having become the home of so many people who hold anti-Semitic ideas, it has become mainstream. I too have begun to feel unsafe in Britain. Some political commentators are now openly saying that "Labour is a racist party." With the election of the new Labour leader, Sir Keir Starmer (2020), he has attempted to repair the damage done during the Jeremy Corbyn years. Yet there is still a long way to go in healing the relationship with the Jewish community in Britain, and particularly those former disaffected members who left the Labour Party.

3 — Prejudice: anti-Zionism/anti-Semitism: A new face of an old hate

Incidents of anti-Semitism have become a global phenomenon. In a recent article written in 2018, Rohr Jewish Learning Institute discusses the modern phenomena of anti-Zionism and anti-Semitism in which the author says that it is a new face of an old hate. It is an historic fact that Israel was established by Jews and, "as such, Israel and Jews are intrinsically linked." Despite whatever an individual Jew's political leanings may be, whether they are of the political left or right, "anyone identifiable as a Jew today is open to an attack that is Anti-Zionist in content." Anti-Semitic attacks are on the increase and this is particularly the case when Israel is in the news.

The number of anti-Semitic attacks is increasing significantly and, from the records of the USA based Anti-Defamation League, here is a sample of some recent attacks:

> Berkeley, CA: The phrase "Zionists should be sent to the gas chamber" was found in a campus restroom not long after a swastika was found on a university owned building."

> New York, NY: "Anti-Semitic slogans were chanted at a protest at CUNY-Hunter College in Manhattan after organisers on Facebook called for participants to oppose the school's 'Zionist administration'. Protesters, who ostensibly gathered to fight for free tuition and other benefits, shouted, 'Zionists out of CUNY! Zionists out of CUNY!'"

Brussels – "A Belgian municipal security officer posted an anti-Semitic rant on Facebook. He wrote: 'The word Jew itself is dirty. If I were in Israel, frankly, I would do to the Jews what they do with the Palestinians – slaughter each and every one of them.' October 20, 2015."

Malmo – "Pro-Palestinian demonstrators chanted 'slaughter the Jews, stab soldiers' during an anti-Israel rally."

The Rohr article continues, "Many incidents of modern anti-Semitism are perpetuated by Moslems and include Anti-Zionistic language even when aimed at targets not connected to Israel in any direct manner: Synagogues, cemeteries, and random Jewish pedestrians. Anti-Zionist sermons are preached in mosques and Islamic bookshops sell Hitler's book *Mein Kampf*." (Rohr Jewish Learning Institute, 2018)

In Germany and France, with the influx of Moslem refugees from the Middle East, North Africa and Asia, there is an exponential increase of anti-Semitism being directed at Germany's Jewish population. Germany is seeking ways to address this problem by introducing diversity awareness training for new citizens and particularly focusing on the problem of Moslem anti-Semitic attitudes towards Jews. The training includes the need for racial, religious and social tolerance and cohesion.

With the 2020 Covid-19 outbreak and pandemic, in a recent survey at Oxford University, UK, one in five English people believe that the Jews are responsible for manufacturing the virus. You may ask what is the basis of such an assumption? This mentality is not dissimilar to blaming the Jews for the 'black-death.'

Israel singled out

Professor Irwin Cotler points out that Israel is the only state that saw terrorism against it officially sanctioned (as resistance to occupation). He points out that Israel has become a pariah state among other states, like the Jew was among his neighbours all through history: "The convening, in December 2001, of the Contracting Parties to the 1949 Geneva Convention on international humanitarian law was a particularly egregious discriminatory act."

Israel is singled out for censure and ridicule, while the Nigerian, Cambodian, Balkan, Rwandan, Sierra Leonean and Democratic Republic of the Congo genocides and killing fields are all but ignored. However, "for 52 years, the first and, to date, only time that the contracting parties have ever come together to put a country in the dock was in the immediate aftermath of the 2001 World Conference against Racism in Durban, South Africa. That country, again, was Israel, an offensive singling-out that undermined the whole regime of international humanitarian law." This says nothing about the historic Turkish genocide against the Armenians and Zimbabwe genocide of the Ndebele under Mugabe.[8]

Together Against Antisemitism

These are difficult and challenging times to live in as a Jew or as someone who loves Israel for many will falsely accuse one of being racist and one finds oneself constantly having to defend Israel's right to exist. A social media campaign, "Together Against Antisemitism," is seeking to raise awareness among the public at large about the scourge of anti-Semitism, which is not only a historic fact, but is a present reality. It is also a rallying call to all those who love the Jewish people and who wish to join their voices to say, "Never again!"[9]

Children of Abraham

Forgetfulness is not only something that afflicts Jews, but all humanity is diminished when people forget where they have come from This is part of the malady faced by the three Abrahamic faiths: Jews, Christians, and Moslems are not immune. For just as they share a common past, so they have a destiny that is intertwined. Due to growing world-wide hostility and religious intolerance, there are times when as a Jew it is wise to hide one's identity. By the wearing of the Star of David, the Chai symbol, special clothes such as the kippah and tzitzit (ceremonial fringes) or some other badge, one identifies oneself as part of that group. This may lay one open to the possibility of an anti-Semitic attack that sometimes includes verbal abuse or physical assault.

On the other hand, to display cultural apparel helps to signify to others that one is Jewish or someone who wants to be associated with the Jewish people. Jewish people are not the only ones who face these challenges. Moslems equally face Islamophobic abuse and attacks when they dress wearing their distinctive clothing, such as women wearing the burka or hijab or the Moslem men wearing the skull cap or religious kaftan. Also, their physical appearance helps to mark them out as part of that group. Christians also, at times, face persecution by wearing a cross necklace. Any overt witness to their faith in the face of secularisation in the Western world equally lays them open to ridicule and victimisation. With this rise of xenophobia, Jews and Moslems each face their own unique problems and instead of opposing each other over the Israeli–Palestinian conflict, they need to offer increasing support and solidarity in the rising tide of race hate directed at both people-groups. There are numerous examples where Jewish and Moslem people face the same pressure from a secular humanistic society that seeks to prohibit religious observance including male circumcision and Jewish kosher (*shechitah* is the Hebrew term for the ritual slaughtering of animals according to the kashrut laws) and Moslem halal ritual slaughter.

The sons and daughters of the three Abrahamic faiths need to remember that God's blessing was for both Isaac and his decedents, as well as Ishmael and his offspring. Though different, nonetheless each of these blessings carry great significance. And in Yeshua all humanity, Jews and Gentiles, are invited to enjoy the blessing that God promised to Abraham. For in him all will be blessed.

Keep talking

Roni Mechanic

Menorah – Bible Land's Museum, Jerusalem, Israel
image by Roni Mechanic©

4 — The different faces of Jesus

One of the aspects concerning peoples' quest to discover who Jesus of Nazareth is and, concerning his human context, is the different faces of Jesus. That also includes his physical appearance and the colour of his skin. Who were his family? Where did he grow up and live his life? Was his physical appearance important? These questions are not of cardinal importance, yet they do help to shape the perception people have of him.

We have some examples such as an image of a black Jesus, a dark complexioned African-looking man. These types of depictions of him have been around from early times. Another image made out of mosaics was discovered of a dark-skinned man with Caucasian features. There are a number of Ethiopian Orthodox icons of a black Jesus in the style of the Ethiopian church. In contrast is the Western European depiction of him as a blond or brown haired, blue eyed person looking like a hippie of the 1960s, as depicted by Hollywood. But is this what he really looked like?

Does this kind of representation of Jesus create a problem for people coming from different cultural heritages? The issue that we are confronted with is that people from other cultures will find him unattractive due to their diverse culture. The millions of Africans taken as slaves were confronted by a white skinned Christ in the lands of their captivity and enslavement. This led to these slaves being alienated due to the cruelty and brutality of their slave masters. But surely, he should have been shown as the poor and oppressed Christ and not the Jesus of the rich and powerful? So, what should Jesus look like? Let us not forget, the reason for his coming into the world was to open the way for people to have an encounter with God. While his physical appearance has some significance, it is not of paramount importance.

The Bible does not actually give a description of Yeshua, except in Revelation 1:12-16.[1]

> Then I turned to see the voice that was speaking to me, and on turning I saw seven golden lampstands, [13]and in the midst of the lampstands one like a son of man, clothed with a long robe and with a golden sash around his chest. [14]The hairs of his head were white, like white wool, like snow. His eyes were like a flame of fire, [15] his feet were like burnished bronze, refined in a furnace, and his voice was like the roar of many waters. [16]In his right hand he held seven stars, from his mouth came a sharp two-edged sword, and his face was like the sun shining in full strength. (ESV)

So, according to this description Jesus is portrayed in a glorified state. Then there is an early third century image of Jesus found in the catacombs of Rome around about 375 C.E. The early believers were reluctant to make representation of Jesus due to the Torah's prohibition in the Ten Commandments of making physical portrayals of humans and beasts lest they become objects of worship as the pagans did – "Thou shalt not make unto thee any graven images." (Exodus 20:4-6 KJV)

This catacomb image of Jesus is of someone dressed in the robes of a Greek or Roman philosopher and the reason for such a portrayal was to indicate that Jesus has surpassed any of those Greek or Roman philosophers. This particular image has included the two Greek letters of the Alpha and the Omega, the first and last letters of the Greek alphabet:

AΩ

Revelation 1:8 (NIV), "I am the Alpha and the Omega," says the Lord God, "who is, and who was, and who is to come, the Almighty."

These two Greek letters were included by the artist to indicate that Jesus was far more important than any of the philosophers of the ancient world. He was not a philosopher, but he was in fact the theologian that correctly interpreted the Torah as the Word made flesh. He is the first and the last, and the most important one.

Before attempting to establishing his identity, I wish to consider who he is not, because the many false impressions distort who Jesus is and have a great bearing on the difficulty of encountering this Jesus. After all, had Jesus not asked, "Who do you say that I am?" (Matthew 16:13-17 NRSV)

He is not an Indian guru seated in the lotus position; he is not an Aryan god as portrayed by the Nazis; he is not a Rastafarian Jesus with dreadlocks and all; he is not a South American revolutionary looking like Che Guevara; he is none of these.

But who then is this Jesus? While it is well established that Jesus is meant to have a universal appeal, we must not forget that, in his original context, he was a first century Jewish man, according to his humanity.

Yeshua first and foremost is a Jew who grew up in a Jewish context and among his own people the Jews. To emphasise his Jewishness, it is helpful to once again visit the quote of Rabbi Dr. Leo Baeck:

> In all his traits, Jesus is through and through a genuinely Jewish character. Such a man as he could only grow up on the soil of Judaism; only there and nowhere else. Jesus [Yeshua] a genuine Jewish personality; all his driving and acting, his bearing and feeling, his speech and his silence, all of it bear the Jewish stamp, the imprint of… the best that was found in Judaism.[10]

Historically, according to sound biblical doctrine, Yeshua is clearly a Jewish man. His earthly existence was beyond doubt that of a Jew, as declared by Rabbi Leo Baeck in the above quotation that we have just considered. What then is all the fuss about if this is a proven historical fact?

While history shows an aspect of the humanity of Yeshua, it is, however, a far more complex issue to determine the significance of his teaching and that of his disciples. This is due to the implications of the universality of the gospel message. If he had simply been an inspired Galilean Jewish teacher that would have a very parochial application. There would probably have been little if any wider interest. Things worked out very differently as history has shown. The Apostles and disciples took the "Great Commission" as a mandate to proclaim the gospel to the ends of the earth:

Luke 24 [44]"Then he said to them, …[46] "… Thus it is written, that the Messiah is to suffer and to rise from the dead on the third day, [47]and that repentance and forgiveness of sins is to be proclaimed in his name to all nations, beginning from Jerusalem. [48]You are witnesses of these things. [49]And see, I am sending upon you what my Father promised; so stay here in the city until you have been clothed with power from on high." (NRSV)

Acts 1 [8] "But you will receive power when the Holy Spirit has come upon you; and you will be my witnesses in Jerusalem, in all Judea and Samaria, and to the ends of the earth." (NRSV)

The Messianic/Christian faith did not remain an obscure Jewish sect. It has continued to grow, and it has become a movement of great significance. There are close on two billion people alive today that, to varying degrees, identify themselves as followers of Jesus of Nazareth. It is all the more important that we endeavour to discover who Yeshua really is. There are various facets to our quest to discover the *'real'* and *'authentic'* Jesus. This is particularly the case in the light of some of the gross distortions of his image.

In using the term 'image', I am not primarily concerned about his physically appearance. 'Image' is a metaphor for the likeness and a description of his character, ethnic, cultural, ancestral and religious heritage. This is the primary consideration of this study. My main concern is to discover who he *was, is and ever* shall be. The spiritual implication of how these questions are answered will have a profound impact upon not only Jews but, equally, the whole Gentile world as well. It will help to answer the question that Yeshua asked his disciples: "Who do you say that I am?" (See Mark 8:29). While others may have an opinion, the personal response to this question can be life changing.

Roni Mechanic

Susannah Heschel's book
"The Aryan Jesus"

(ISBN-13: 9780691148052, 978-0691148052)

5 — The Aryan Jesus

It is one thing to seek to 'rebrand' Yeshua to be culturally appropriate, yet it is quite another thing to distort his image way beyond a straightforward desire to contextualise him. It is very important that the gospel message should be best understood within a particular cultural ethos. Yet it is a completely different thing that the Aryan Jesus is a dreadful distortion of who Yeshua HaMashiach (Jesus the Messiah) truly is.

Susannah Heschel, the daughter of the famous Jewish theologian Dr Abraham Heschel says that, in Nazi Germany with the rise to power of National Socialism in 1933, "THE INSTITUTE (Dates: 1932-1945) for the Study and Eradication of Jewish Influence on German Church Life, was established." Its objective was to purge Christianity of all Jewish augmentation and influences.[11]

During the nineteenth century particularly, German theologians were attempting to develop a contemporary paradigm of the person of Jesus. This movement became part of what became known as "the Jesus' Quest," in which they attempted to explain the difference between the Jesus of history, a first century Jew, and the Jesus of faith. With the growing turmoil in Europe in the 1930's the desire to discover a Jesus whose image complied with this new nationalistic spirit in Germany was being sought. Among others, the theological work of Rudolf Bultmann was being referenced in the face of the rising nationalism.

The prominent German theologian, Rudolf Bultmann, was a member of the Confessing Church and critical towards National Socialism. He spoke out against the mistreatment of Jews, against nationalistic excesses and against the dismissal of non-Aryan Christian ministers. He did not, however, speak out against "the anti-Semitic laws which had already been promulgated" and he was philosophically limited in his ability to "repudiate, in a comprehensive manner, the central tenets of Nazi racism and anti-Semitism." Consequently, he proved to be a mixed blessing. While the reason for him not being able to repudiate the central tenets of Nazi racism and anti-Semitism are not clear, his attitude towards Judaism as a religion does appear to be a spiritual resurrection of Marcionism.[12]

Alas, it resonated and struck a chord with THE INSTITUTE "That Jesus was not a Jew was the ultimate Western fantasy,"… It was also the secret hope of a strain of Christian theology since the days of the second-century Christian theologian Marcion, who rejected the Old Testament and its God… From Marcion [to Bultmann and then] to Grundmann, the de-Judaization of Christianity was rooted in the conundrum of Christian supersession :.."[13]

On this subject of the de-Judaization of Christianity, Rudolf Bultmann, as stated, was clearly not a Nazi and to accuse him of holding to what the Aryan Christians stood for would be wrong. However, the theological assertions about Jesus and his Jewishness, and the progression from his theological stance about Judaism are only a few steps away from THE INSTITUTE'S Aryan Jesus. Bultmann said, "for the Christian the Old Testament is not revelation but is essentially related to God's revelation in Christ as hunger is to food, and despair is to hope… The God who spoke to Israel no longer speaks to us in the time of the new

Covenant." No one can blame Bultmann for the Nazi racial theories nor can he be held responsible for the portrayal of Jesus as an enemy of the Jews. He never said anything remotely like the Nazi's nor participated in their heinous crimes against Jews, Judaism and the Jewish Jesus. Bultmann quotes the Nazi theologian Albert Rosenberg's description of Jesus: "the great personality of Jesus," has "been misused," by ecclesiastical Christianity. Whatever its original form, the great personality of Jesus Christ was immediately after his departure burdened and amalgamated with all the rubbish of Near Eastern, of Jewish and African life."[14] Bultmann was ambivalent towards the Jewishness of Jesus.

Bultmann says, this "perspective that is expressed in such statements (made by Albert Rosenberg) is not new. It was earnestly discussed by the theological research of the preceding generation after it had been particularly brought to attention by Wilhelm Wrede's *Paulus* (1905). According to Wrede, Paul should be considered the second founder of Christianity; "as the real creator of Christian theology, it was he who made Christianity into a religion of redemption."[15] Bultmann's ideas that he expressed in 1936 were part of the mentality that came to characterise the German Christian movement progressively. It built on the earlier ideas of previous generations of Christian theologians that held those negative attitudes towards Judaism and consequently sought to divorce Jesus from his Jewish context and heritage.

What does an Aryan Jesus look like? The process of purging Christianity of its Jewish heritage as advocated by Walter Grundmann, together with other members of THE INSTITUTE, put forward the argument that Jesus was not a Jew but, rather, he had sought the deconstruction of Judaism. These suggestions were based on arguments that had been put forward long before 1939, when THE INSTITUTE was established. These comprised a mixture of political, social and theological ideas and included racial theories that emerged in the nineteenth century in Europe. These included ideas about language and religions that were seen as "a manifestation of race."

This purge of the so-called 'rubbish' of Near Eastern, of Jewish and African life, that had burdened and amalgamated with the life of Jesus and early Christianity, was carried through as ruthlessly as the Final Solution to break any link with Jesus and his Jewish heritage. They held that Jesus' religious teaching originated in Hellenism, Buddhism, Hinduism, and Zoroastrianism – "anything but Judaism." On closer scrutiny their arguments would not stand up to any scholars worth their salt. Typical of this brand of scholarship, the arguments were weak and the sources that they based them upon were all but non-existent. Through their spurious methodology, Jesus was transformed from a Jew prefigured in the Hebrew Scriptures into an anti-Semite and proto-Nazi.

According to Thomas Howard, "Instead of the Old Testament prefiguring Christ… Christ himself came to prefigure, or legitimise, various forms of Christian cultural awareness." "Jesus became a prefiguration for Nazi Germany's fight against the Jews," according to THE INSTITUTE.[16] In their effort to radicalise Europe, Nazi Germany rejected Jesus' Jewishness and affirmed that he was an Aryan. These racial theories held that Jesus was an idealised "White Man," and this in turn encouraged

European male Caucasians to fantasise and view themselves as "Christ." He was not imagined as a Jew, but an Aryan. Here we also witness elements of Nietzsche's ÜBERMENSCH – SUPERMAN.

Ernest Renan, in his attempt to rebrand Jesus by his racialization of him, through his "studies of Semitic languages, did claim that monotheism stemmed from a Semitic instinct, while Indo-Europeans were by nature polytheistic." However, he chose to portray Semitic grammar as being rigid. He claimed it as the "barrenness and monotony of Semitic culture, [lacking] philosophy, science, and art," and that it was consequently hindered in "growth, creativity, and imagination," giving rise to an absolutism lacking in imagination that is characteristic of mythology, and lacking in Judaism and Islam.[17]

Renan's contrasting of the Semitic that he portrayed as possessing negative qualities, and the Aryan that was not only shown as being positive, but also the root of Christianity, grew stronger during his career from his research in 1857 *Studies in Religious History* and his subsequent five-volume *History of the People of Israel* (1888-1896). In this work, "language, race, culture and religion became interchangeable." He contrasted Semitic (Jews and Arabs), with Aryans, whom he identified with Greeks, Indians, and Germans. This led him to replacing Greek with "Aryan," which became the functioning term for his contrasting and superseding "Hebraism" with "Hellenism." These racial theories long dominated the European intellectual discourse. Renan's depiction "of Jesus as a Galilean, who underwent a transformation from Jew to Christian," well suited the Nazis and THE INSTITUTE who capitalised and developed his linguistic, cultural, racial and religious theories about Jesus,

Judaism and Christianity. (Heschel S, 2008:34) In his attempts to fashion and rebrand a Jesus who bears nothing of his original Jewish identity, Renan used faulty reasoning.

Dietrich Bonhoeffer and Ben Witherington III

Dietrich Bonhoeffer of the Confessing Church reacted strongly as a consequence of the 7th April 1933 Aryan laws which were distinctly anti-Jewish. When it became clear that Jewish Christians and Christians in mixed marriages with Jews were to be expelled from the church, he raised serious questions challenging the German Christians:

"We are in no way concerned with the question whether our members of German stock can continue to share responsibility with Jews for the communion of the Church. Rather, it is the task of the Christian proclamation to say, 'here, where Jew and German stand together under God's word, is the Church, here it is proven whether or not the Church is still the Church.'"[18]

Ben Witherington III in *The Jesus Quest: The Third Search for the Jew of Nazareth*, says, "In the middle and late nineteenth century in Europe, as one of the final effects of the Enlightenment, historical-critical scholarship began to be applied in earnest to Gospel narratives, with a number of academics writing 'new summaries of the life of Jesus'." (Witherington III, p 9) Some of these efforts were more of a sensationalist appeal, not based upon any new facts that had come to light but were rather because of the new way of reading of the Canonical Gospels.

David Friedrich Strauss was one of the foremost of these scholars, in his large work, *"Das Leben Jesu"* (1835-36), Witherington says, "This work was a clarion call for 'unbiased' historical research to be done on the life of Jesus." (Witherington III, 1997:9) Following Strauss' groundbreaking work, Joseph Ernest Renan's *Vie de Jesus – The Life of Jesus* (1860's - p 9), is an example of the new field of research that was developing followed by Albert Schweitzer, *The Quest for the Historical Jesus*. The contrast between Schweitzer and Renan becomes apparent. Schweitzer was to reject Renan's racial theories and his work was seminal in the development in the "Jesus Quest," while Renan had an axe to grind with his desire to separate Jesus from his Hebraic roots and heritage.[19]

A "weaponised" Jesus

A Jewish response to this type of de-Judaization of Yeshua and Christianity has a two-fold impact. On the one hand, there are those Jewish people that readily encourage Jesus to be seen as a non-Jewish, Gentile god. He can then be relegated to the margins and together with all other non-Jewish gurus, messiahs and deities, he will have little if any significance to Jews and Judaism.

On the other hand, there are those Jewish and Christian scholars and theological thinkers that are deeply troubled by the type of thinking that produced an Aryan Jesus. This is because he has been "weaponised" and used against Jews and Judaism with the devastating consequences that most recent and past history have shown. By portraying Jesus Christ as an enemy of the Jewish people, the Nazis sought justification for their war against these enemies of god. Yet this 'Aryan god,' is not the God of the Hebrew Scriptures, nor is he the God of the New Testament. Possibly a Marcionite god, but most certainly not a Jewish God who loves Israel and the Jewish people. He equally loves all humankind.

A Messianic Jewish perspective

A Messianic Jewish perspective gives a vital ingredient to redress the theological distortions and imbalances that characterise both Christian and Jewish attitudes towards Yeshua.

Firstly, for those Jewish believers who love and wish to affirm their Jewish identity, it is of paramount importance that a Jewish "Jesus" is portrayed. This is not done as some accuse them, in order to entice unwitting and naïve Jews who are ignorant and uninformed about their own faith.

Secondly, and more importantly, it is not theologically unsound or without justification to portray a "Jewish Jesus." In his original context he was born and lived as a Jew and saw his calling primarily to his fellow Jews. In Matthew 15:24 (NRSV) "He answered, 'I was sent only to the lost sheep of the house of Israel.'" Gratefully, there are both Christian and Jewish scholars who concur with this assertion about him. To this discussion we now turn.

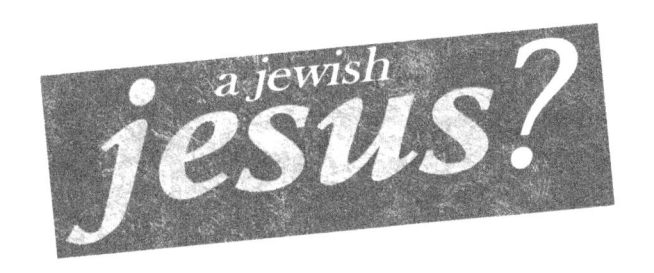

a jewish jesus?

6 — A Jewish view of Yeshua

Albert Schweitzer celebrated Jesus' Jewishness. Schweitzer's image of Jesus is a total negation of the Nazi aberration and distortion of who he is. Schweitzer, as one of the pioneers of the Jesus Quest, emphasised Jesus' humanity placing him in his first century Jewish context.

Despite Protestant Christianity's dogmatic assertion of "sola scriptura" (only Scripture) as the basis for establishing sound doctrine, and the fact that the church should have protected it from de-Judaization, many Protestant theologians "succumbed to an individualistic Hellenised conception of the Christian tradition, to a romanticised oversimplification of the problem of faith and inwardness, to pantheism and sentimentality. Only a conscious commitment to the roots of Christianity in Judaism could have saved it from such distortions."[20]

Once more Susannah Heschel's insight based on her research of Abraham Geiger's work is helpful:

> "Ultimately, Jesus' Jewishness could not be denied. The only path out of the discomfiting claim was either painting conventional first-century Judaism in repugnant colours or shifting the significance of Jesus as an historical figure from his teaching to his racial identity. The problem of Jesus' Jewishness became tied to significant political developments. With the rise of German nationalism in the nineteenth century, suggestions began to be heard by theologians that Jesus was a Jew by religion, but an Aryan by race. At the

beginning of that century, the philosopher Fichte had proposed the Aryan Christ."[21]

By the time the Nazi's Aryan Jesus was fully developed, his Jewish origin and identity was completely obliterated. Schweitzer asserted that not only did Jesus not hate the Jews, nor was he their implacable enemy; his mission was most certainly not to destroy them as enemies of God. He came to deliver Israel as their Saviour and Messiah.

If Jesus came to deliver Israel then, in my personal quest to discover him it was of great importance to me that he was a Jew. The numerous presentations of Jesus can be very confusing to the genuine seeker. It is not primarily his physical appearance that is important to me, but a much more important matter has to do with who he is.

An unknown image of Jesus: The Son of God

The BBC commissioned Jeremy Bowen, the well-known Middle Eastern correspondent and journalist to undertake a project to explore an unknown image of Jesus, entitled *The Son of God*. The team was given the brief to pursue their investigation from an archaeological, medical and forensic standpoint, and also from a geographical perspective. They were also to search for any artistic images that might throw light on this project. In contrast to the stereotypical image of what a Jewish man may look like, the team discovered a skull of a first century Jewish male and the agreed expert opinion was that the appearance differs substantially to that of today.

The reaction to this reconstruction was varied. While some liked and approved of it, others felt that it was a lavish waste of money and time. A team member, Israeli Jewish archaeologist Joe Zeus said, "In constructing this head, we

are not claiming this is exactly like Jesus' face, we are trying to counteract all the bad images of blond haired, blue eyed Jesuses running around Hollywood productions. Yes, he wasn't the blond haired, blue eyed Jesuses depicted on Easter-cards."[22]

So, who is he?

Is he a Jewish Jesus called Yeshua; or as Rabbi Shmuley Boteach says, is he a "Kosher Jesus"? "Jesus of Nazareth is the most famous Jew who ever lived yet remains profoundly alienated from his own people. At best he is viewed as the founder of a new religion which for millennia was hostile to Judaism. At worst he is seen as the source of the world's anti-Semitism, with the charge that the Jews were responsible for his death being the impetus for the murder of countless Jews throughout the ages. But the historical Jesus is also foreign to most Christians who are oblivious to the life he lived as a Jew, his real mission in ancient Judea, the source of most of his celebrated teachings, and his firm attachment to his people."[23]

Some say that he is an apostate Jew and a heretic, while others say that he is a sorcerer and magician. In South America Jesus was called a revolutionary by Liberation theologians. Some said that he was married to Mary of Magdala and had a family, while others suggested that he was gay. The Nazis claimed that he is an Aryan Jesus who hated the Jews and had come to destroy them. Some have typecast him as a colonial "white Jesus." The Black Consciousness movement have made him into a black Jesus who is anti-racial segregation, a post-colonial, and post-Apartheid Jesus.

Sub-Christian sects such as the Jehovah's Witness, Christadelphians, and Mormons have fashioned him after their own distorted, non-biblical outlook; while for others such as the Moslems, he is a prophet. Hindus say he is one of the incarnations of the god Krishna; and for some he is an esoteric Jesus of Gnosticism, Theosophical and Anthroposophical (Rudolf Steiner) imagining. The "True Jews," who are spiritualist, call Jesus the Great Medium, and the Rosicrucians and Swedenborgians (New Church) cast him according to their occult teaching.

Is he "Jesus of Arabia?" Yes, but is he the *Jewish Jesus of Arabia* or is he rather a *Palestinian liberation Jesus* who fights against Israel and downplays his Jewish identity? The cinema portrays him as a fool in the *Life of Brian* and in the Amazon Prime film *Preacher* he is portrayed as a demented and deluded idiot. Other possibilities suggest that he is a lunatic, liar or deceiver. This list is by no means exhaustive.

How should we view him?

While some claims are clearly foolhardy and hardly worthy of serious consideration, other claims do justify further consideration. Yet, how are we to view him with so many competing claims? An important place to begin our exploration is the New Testament scriptures as these give the clearest picture of who he is. The multitude of fanciful and esoteric portrayals of him only serve to obscure his true image, making him either unattractive or irrelevant to the serious enquirer.

Antidote to confusion

The Hebrew Bible, together with the New Testament, are a strong antidote to the considerable confusion about where to find spiritual fulfilment and enlightenment. Abraham Heschel says, in the perpetuation of a negative mentality in the modern era there is the "…tendency to look for the spirit everywhere except in the words of Holy Scripture…" (Rothschild, 1990, p. 303). Heschel makes a powerful and earnest plea for Jews and Christians to decide whether to be involved in the Hebrew Bible or live away from it?

The future of the Western world will depend on the way in which we relate ourselves to the Hebrew Bible. The extent that Christians and Jews identify with it is the test of how authentic their faith is. When we fail to identify with the Hebrew Scriptures, the apparent confusion of today is clear, afflicting all seekers.[24]

A solid foundation

A solid foundation is needed and, as Abraham Heschel has said, this need to return to the Hebrew Scriptures is very important. I must add that this must include the New Testament as well. For just as the Hebrew Bible anticipated the coming One, so we discover that he is fully revealed in the person and work of Yeshua, God's only Son. The Scripture says that his coming is of great significance:

John 10:10b, "I have come that they may have life, and have it to the full." (NIV)

While there are many voices that seek to gain people's attention, there is only one voice that we should listen to:

John 10:27, "My sheep hear my voice, and I know them, and they follow me:" (KJV)

My personal quest was not along a straight path, for it did include twists and turns. Some of my endeavours did end up in cul-de-sacs, yet despite the various challenges that I faced, there was an awareness of divine providence that was guiding and directing me along the pathway. Similarly, each of us need to individually make the effort to discover the truth. However, it is clear this is a complex business. It will never be exactly the same as another person's quest, due to the multitude of factors that come into play in helping us to find God's peace and personal fulfilment.

I want to be clear, that I am not advocating a kind of universalism. Rather, what I am saying is how we personally discover that Yeshua is the way.

John 14:6, Jesus answered, "I am the way and the truth and the life. No one comes to the Father except through me" (NIV). This exclusive claim may make us uncomfortable and cause us to want to reject these words that Jesus spoke. The answer as to why he made such an exclusive assertion is due to the theological understanding that he is the true mediator between God and humankind. This is not meant to imply that other's spirituality has no validity, but rather should be understood against other statements that Jesus made:

John 10:9 NIV, "I am the gate/door – (ESV); whoever enters through me will be saved. They will come in and go out and find pasture."

7 — On being Jewish

A rich cultural heritage was imparted to me in my early years, growing up in Johannesburg, with family, the Jewish community, synagogue, and Habonim (The Builders, Zionist Youth Movement), that enhanced the Jewish cycle of life. We eagerly anticipated the Jewish festivals that more than punctuated the year, for they added colour and light to our lives as Jews. Our local synagogue was aligned to the United Hebrew Congregations of the Commonwealth, which is part of mainstream British Orthodox Judaism.

Rites of passage

Rites of passage cover the whole spectrum of life for participating members of the Jewish community, from birth to death. These help to foster a sense of belonging in an often hostile and uncertain world.

Beginning with circumcision and then the *pidyon haben* – Hebrew: פדיון הבן or redemption of the First-born son is a commandment in Judaism whereby a Jewish firstborn son of his mother is "redeemed" by use of silver coins by a Cohen (priest). These two rites are derived explicitly from commandments in the Hebrew Bible.

Images from the Bible linked to marriage and death have evolved into the modern-day way that weddings and funerals are conducted. Bar mitzvah is not mentioned in the Bible, Mishnah, or Talmud, nor has the Bible a ritual of conversion. The development of some of these rituals have also been influenced by Christian and Moslem religious and cultural practices.

"In some circumstances rites of passages have been linked to other biblical-based celebrations such as festivals, pilgrimages... with the personalization of religion that has characterised Western culture, much attention is now paid to the different ways life milestones may be linked to Jewish-tradition."[25]

Joy and sadness — the cup of life

These Jewish cultural and religious celebrations are characterised by *joy* and *sadness*. Not only do Jewish people celebrate the joys of life but also, at times, pause to remember those who have died in the Holocaust, called Yom HaShoah and the Kaddish sacred prayer is said. The Yiskor sacred prayer of remembrance is said four times in the year at Pesach (Passover), Shavuot (Weeks), Yom Kippur (Day of Atonement) and Shemini Atzeret (Eighth Day of Sukkot or Booths). It is said silently with all present standing in the synagogue and its origin dates back to the Crusader era when the Crusaders slaughtered the "Christ Killing" Jews on their way to liberate the Holy Land from the Saracen – Moslems. Personal loss with the death of a loved one is accompanied by the sitting of Shiva which is observed for seven days of mourning when family and friends join with those who are mourning and the Kaddish memorial prayer is recited.

Even at a Jewish wedding, after rejoicing in the marriage of a bride and groom, the ceremony concludes with the groom crushing a glass with his foot. This symbolises the destruction of the Second Temple, introducing a note of solemnity into an otherwise joyous occasion. It may be referred to as the cup of life from which we drink, that is bitter–sweet. For how would we know joy, if there was not sadness? - "Le Chaim – To Life!"

With the Jewish year beginning in September – October, the High and Holy Days, of Rosh Hashanah and Yom Kippur, are quickly followed by Succoth and conclude with Simchat Torah. A word tumble helps to illustrate this season that is sometimes referred to as Trumpets.

The Feast of Trumpets

The year concludes with Hanukkah, celebrating the Maccabean victory against the Greek Seleucids and the assertion of Jewish sovereignty (160-140 B.C.E.). This included the lighting of the Hanukkiah for eight days and the eating of oily foods such as doughnuts and blintzes
(a type of Jewish spring rolls filled with cheese or offal).

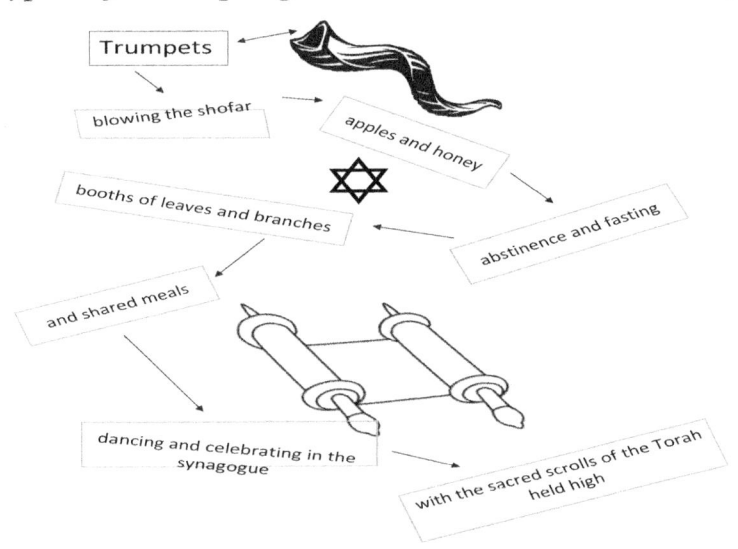

Trumpets
blowing the shofar
apples and honey
booths of leaves and branches
abstinence and fasting
and shared meals
dancing and celebrating in the synagogue
with the sacred scrolls of the Torah held high

Graphic created by Roni Mechanic ©

Around the month of February, the Jewish festival of Purim is celebrated and, though it is attended with fun and festivity with children dressing up in fancy dress, having parties and the eating of special foods, it commemorates the deliverance of the Jewish people from a near act of genocide when wicked Haman sought to destroy the Jews of Persia during the reign of King Ahasuerus. However, they were saved through the wise action of Mordechai the Jew and his niece Queen Esther who intervened on behalf of the Jewish people thwarting the evil plot of Prime Minister Haman.

Purim has particular relevance today in light of modern anti-Semitism and anti-Zionism, with Jewish self-defence and defiance against her enemies.

Circle of Life

Completing the circle of the year with Jewish religious celebration during the months of April – May is the festival of Pesach. Passover recalls the deliverance of the Hebrew nation from the land of bondage and slavery in Egypt when God brought them out with a mighty hand and outstretched arm through his servants Moses and Aaron. This is also known as the Feast of Unleavened Bread. The festival is held mainly in homes and community centres with the holding of the Passover Seder meal and retelling of the story of the Exodus.

Each week is concluded with the celebration of the Sabbath on a Friday evening. The Sabbath starts with the mother of the house kindling the Sabbath lights and the family gathering around the dinner table. Blessings are said by the father over the children; the reading of Proverbs 31:10-31 with him praising his wife; and before the Sabbath meal is served the *Kiddush* is said which is the blessing of wine and bread. (See Sacks J., Authorised Daily Prayer Book, p 311*f*).

In addition, Jewish philanthropy has a long tradition with Jewish people giving significant charitable donations to not only Jewish causes, but also to the wider world. Jews are involved in helping to foster a better understanding among the nations. Jewish contributions go to all aspects of life – science, medicine, philosophy, the arts, theology, inter-faith dialogue and much more.

The Shema

The Shema helps to define Judaism and it holds a central place as a prayer that observant Jews recite twice daily in morning and evening prayer. It is an affirmation of God's uniqueness and by its daily recitation the Jewish worshiper is reminded of the special covenant relationship that God has established with Israel. The prayer's application assists the Jewish worshipper to not only love God, but also to seek to apply his precepts and principles to the whole of one's life. Equally, the importance of this prayer should be taught to one's children. During the day while awake and at night while asleep the practicing of the presence of God should become a constant preoccupation.

Shema - Deuteronomy 6:5-9

שְׁמַע יִשְׂרָאֵל, יְיָ אֱלֹהֵינוּ, יְיָ ׀ אֶחָד:

Roni Mechanic

בָּרוּךְ שֵׁם כְּבוֹד מַלְכוּתוֹ לְעוֹלָם וָעֶד:
וְאָהַבְתָּ אֵת יְיָ אֱלֹהֶיךָ, בְּכָל | לְבָבְךָ, וּבְכָל נַפְשְׁךָ, וּבְכָל מְאֹדֶךָ: וְהָיוּ הַדְּבָרִים הָאֵלֶּה אֲשֶׁר אָנֹכִי מְצַוְּךָ הַיּוֹם, עַל | לְבָבֶךָ: וְשִׁנַּנְתָּם לְבָנֶיךָ וְדִבַּרְתָּ בָּם, בְּשִׁבְתְּךָ בְּבֵיתֶךָ, וּבְלֶכְתְּךָ בַדֶּרֶךְ, וּבְשָׁכְבְּךָ, וּבְקוּמֶךָ: וּקְשַׁרְתָּם לְאוֹת עַל יָדֶךָ, וְהָיוּ לְטֹטָפֹת בֵּין עֵינֶיךָ: וּכְתַבְתָּם עַל מְזֻזוֹת בֵּיתֶךָ, וּבִשְׁעָרֶיךָ:

* בָּרוּךְ שֵׁם כְּבוֹד מַלְכוּתוֹ לְעוֹלָם וָעֶד

Baruch shem kavod malchuto l'olam va-ed

* Blessed is the name of His glorious kingdom for ever and ever. (This sentence is added as a liturgical response when said in worship).

DEUTERONOMY 6:4-9 (NRSV)
[4] Hear, O Israel: The LORD is our God, the LORD alone. [5] You shall love the LORD your God with all your heart, and with all your soul, and with all your might. [6] Keep these words that I am commanding you today in your heart. [7] Recite them to your children and talk about them when you are at home and when you are away, when you lie down and when you rise. [8] Bind them as a sign on your hand, fix them as an emblem on your forehead, [9] and write them on the doorposts of your house and on your gates.

This prayer not only declares one's trust in the true and living God, but also encompasses the whole of life. This is also the last prayer that a Jewish person says at the point of death.

Not a stranger

I am no stranger to Jewish festivities and celebrations and, together with my family and friends, we eagerly anticipated the holding of these special markers, helping to remind us of who we are as Jews, our place in the world and longing to understand God's purpose in calling us his 'Chosen People." In Fidler on the Roof, Tevye the dairyman is having a rather bad day as his horse is sick and he has to pull his milk cart along to deliver the milk to his customers in the Russian village of Anatevka in the Pale of settlement. He raises his gaze heavenwards and acclaims, "God, we know that we are the Chosen People. Would you mind choosing someone else for a change?"

Being a Jew is a cause of wonderment and perplexity in which I too have contemplated what it means to be a member of the Chosen People, particularly when it comes to our suffering and equally pondered as to what is our destiny?

Heritage

The rich heritage that characterises Jewish life was born in antiquity with the history of ancient Israel. The telling of the Jewish narrative is an epic story. In the present, being a Jewish person increasingly has its existential challenges. The future, while yet unknown from a human viewpoint, looks dangerous and foreboding. The rise of anti-Semitism, the volatility of the Middle East, Iran, Hezbollah, Hamas all calling for Israel's destruction are a cause for deep concern but not alarm.

However, from a biblical perspective, there are many promises that the God of Israel will not abandon his ancient people. While many things in our contemporary world do not offer security, this is a cause of hope. He has promised to restore Israel to their ancient land and bless them. We read in Deuteronomy 30:3-5 (NRSV), [3] "Then the Lord your God will restore your fortunes and have compassion on you, gathering you again from all the peoples among whom the Lord your God has scattered you. [4] Even if you are exiled to the ends of the world, from there the Lord your God will gather you, and from there he will bring you back. [5] The Lord your God will bring you into the land that your ancestors possessed, and you will possess it; he will make you more prosperous and numerous than your ancestors."

The return of the Jews to the land of Israel and the establishment of the Jewish state in 1948 is a wonderful fulfilment of the passage from Deuteronomy 30.

In those days of the Messianic Kingdom all will be changed: "It will come to pass in the latter days [the days of Messiah] that the mountain of the Lord's Temple will be established as the highest mountain and will be exalted above the hills and all nations will stream towards it. And many peoples will say, 'Come, let us go up to the mountain of the Lord, to the House of the God of Jacob, and He will teach us His ways and we will walk in His paths'; for from Zion instruction will go forth, and the Message of the Lord from Jerusalem; and He will act as international arbiter for the nations and will rebuke many peoples. And they will beat their swords into ploughshares and their spears into scythes. A nation will no longer raise a sword against other nations, nor will they ever again learn to make war." (Isaiah 2:1-4 - NRSV).

All Israel shall be saved

Romans11: [25] I do not want you to be ignorant of this mystery, brothers, so that you will not be conceited: A hardening in part has come to Israel, until the full number of the Gentiles has come in. [26] And so all Israel will be saved, as it is written:

"The Deliverer will come from Zion; He will remove godlessness from Jacob. [27] And this is My covenant with them when I take away their sins." (NRSV).

There is a two-fold aspect to the question of God's promise of blessing upon the Jewish people: As discussed, the question of the restoration of Israel involves an ingathering of Jewish people to the land of their forefathers and this saw the rebirth of Jewish hope with the founding of the Zionist movements in the mid to late nineteenth century. Aliyah which means literally 'going up' to the Land of Israel is a constant theme repeated throughout the Hebrew Scriptures. The modern state of Israel celebrated its seventieth year of existence in May 2018 since its establishment in 1948. Jewish people from more than 100 nations have regathered in the 'Promised Land.' Though many people contest Israel's right to exist, including a number of Christians, there is an overwhelming number of Christians who actively support Israel as a sovereign nation.

Equally, there are a minority of Jewish people who question whether there should be a Jewish state. Some do so for religious reasons, asserting that only the Messiah has the right to set up a Jewish state when he will come to rule in the earth. And there are also Jewish people on the hard, political left who are anti-Zionist, who hold that Israel is illegitimate as it stole the land from the Palestinians.

So, who does the land belong to? I believe that God has the last word, because according to the Scriptures if he fails to keep his promises to Israel, then how can God be relied on to fulfil any other of his promises, not only to the Jews, but all humanity? Those Christians who reject this are motivated by replacementism and also hold to the belief that God is finished with the Jews because of their rejection of Jesus as the Messiah. This is not only theologically unsound, but also expresses an antipathy towards Jews, Judaism and Israel.

Graphic created by Roni Mechanic ©

8 — Who is this Yeshua?

Friends and foes alike have a lot to say about who Jesus is. Yeshua asked his disciples, "Who do people say that I am?"– Mark 8:22-38 (NIV).

MATTHEW 16:14-16 (NIV),
[14] They replied, "Some say John the Baptist; others say Elijah; and still others, Jeremiah or one of the prophets." [15] "But what about you?" he asked. "Who do you say I am?"[16] Simon Peter answered, "You are the Messiah, the Son of the living God."

Alas, no such clarity is easily given. Even as Peter had this moment of insightful revelation, in the very next breath he loses the plot when Jesus tells them that that he must fulfil his destiny and be put to death in Jerusalem.

MATTHEW 16:22-23 (NIV),
[22] Peter took him aside and began to rebuke him. "Never, Lord!" he said. "This shall never happen to you!" [23] Jesus turned and said to Peter, "Get behind me, Satan! You are a stumbling block to me; you do not have in mind the concerns of God, but merely human concerns."

There is little wonder that there are so many different images of Jesus that portray the underlying different perceptions that people have of him. Over the years, I have encountered a great diversity of opinions about who he is, who he is claimed to be and even what he looked like.

Due to the fact that Jesus' earthly existence took place over 2000 years ago, in answer to the multiple questions that surround the person of Jesus of Nazareth, both individual and group perceptions and portrayals of him are complex.

These often reflect more about the one who is seeking to unravel the mystery of Jesus, than about Jesus himself. Folk bring with them all their preconceptions, prejudices, confusion and doubts about him.

We should note that with Peter's declaration about Jesus, part of Jesus reply includes a very important statement:

[16]"Simon Peter answered, "You are the Messiah, the Son of the living God." [17] And Jesus answered him, "Blessed are you, Simon son of Jonah! For flesh and blood has not revealed this to you, but my Father in heaven.""

The question of divine revelation is fundamental to answering the very complex issues that surround the person of Yeshua HaMashiach and we will most certainly return to this throughout this endeavour in our consideration of my personal quest to encounter Yeshua.

A Jewish viewpoint

While it is an encouraging development that Jewish scholars are willing to consider the question as to who Jesus of Nazareth is, their quest is not without its problems. There are fault lines and a red line that Jews are not willing to cross while still being considered to be Jewish.

The highly esteemed Jewish scholar and theologian, Dr. Geza Vermes devoted many years endeavouring to place Jesus in his original Jewish context. He portrays him as an outstanding enigmatic Jewish character but, for him, he can never be the divine Son of God of Christian dogma and confession. He made a radical division between the Jewish

Jesus of history and the Jesus of faith as held by those that he refers to as Christian fundamentalists. He conjectures that the only source that we have for constructing the historic Jesus is the Gospel accounts. He argues these are largely a construction of Christian origin that sought to portray Jesus as the Messiah of Jewish hope. For a Jew, Jesus cannot be accepted as anything other than an extra-ordinary Jew. He quotes Rudolf Bultmann, a liberal early twentieth century German theologian who, in contrast to "the fundamentalists," says that no attempt should be made for a quest for the historic Jesus. "We can now know almost nothing concerning the life and personality of Jesus, since the early Christian sources show no interest in either."[27]

No one is an island

Dr. Vermes is in good company with the liberal Protestant theologian Rudolf Bultmann and the Catholic theologian Eduard Schillebeeckx who equally sought a division between the Jesus of history and the Jesus of faith. No doubt Dr. Vermes was aware of these Christian theologians and their liberal approach to the person of Jesus Christ, giving him license to follow their line of thinking about who Jesus of Nazareth is.

Dr. Pinchas Lapide makes an important contribution to the quest for the historic Jesus in his book, *The Resurrection of Jesus*. He asks an important question based upon the Apostle Paul's provocative question in 1 Corinthians 1:13, "Has Christ been divided? Was Paul crucified for you? Or were you baptised in the name of Paul?" and, as Lapide eloquently shows there seems to be a division of Jesus the Nazarene into two – an earthly Jesus who is of no theological significance as regards the history of salvation –

heilsgschichte[28]: an interpretation of history emphasizing God's saving acts and viewing Jesus Christ as central in redemption and an ascended heavenly Christ.[29]

Dr Lapide says that it is of the utmost importance that Yeshua is a Jew, through and through. "I would never have contemplated having anything to do with a Gentile god, nor any other strange distortions of him."

Jesus' Jewishness is powerfully affirmed by Rabbi Pinchas Lapide. He says, "The historical Jesus... was born as a Jew, was circumcised, educated, and lived his whole earthly life among Jews, his ministry, preaching and teaching being limited to the physical nation of Israel." However, "It is completely different with the post-Easter Christ who as a heavenly figure of light as a "Masked God," as Eduard Schillebeeckx ironically calls this construction, has nothing at all to do with his birth in Judaism or with our earth"

So, which is it to be?

"The historical Jesus" of Lapide's imaging, or the "Masked God" and ascended Christ of Schillebeeckx's construction, or is it possible that there is a third option of the Jewish Jesus who is both Messiah of Jewish hope and Saviour of humankind?

Dr. Lapide convincingly argues that the resurrection appearances of Jesus as recorded in the New Testament all took place in a Jewish context and "emphasise not only the bodily identity of the Risen One, but also his unbroken identity with the same Jesus of Nazareth whose life and strife was devoted to his people Israel."[30] Furthermore, all his appearances were exclusively to Jews and there are no recorded Gentile witnesses to these events. Lapide enumerates those who encountered the risen Jesus – the three Mary's, a group of apostles, the disciples on the Emmaus road; "the more than five hundred brethren" as related by Paul. Peter also said in the Temple portico, "God having raised up his servant, sent him to you first, to bless you." (Acts 3.26) We may conclude that the Risen One's coming was specifically to bless Israel. Dr. Lapide holds a much more conservative outlook to the question of the resurrection of Jesus than many liberal Christian theologians do.

In addition, as Lapide says, whatever one may want to conclude about the Easter event was that it "was primarily and chiefly a Jewish faith experience."[31] The whole thing "came into existence – just as Jesus himself – in the midst of the people of Israel and spread from there over the whole world."[32] Eduard Schillebeeckx and Rudolf Bultmann clearly had another agenda and theological outlook to Dr. Lapide, whose assertion put him much closer to an orthodox Christian position than to that of the Liberal German theological thinking of the late nineteenth and early twentieth century.

Perplexity is one of the problems that face our human existence. This is equally the case when one is attempting to discover who the real Yeshua is. When Christian theologians hold such contrary viewpoints, how is the genuine Jewish seeker to arrive at a knowledge of the truth? What is clear in our quest is that there is a great diversity of opinion concerning many aspects of the person and work of Yeshua.

Roni Mechanic

The true agenda

The true agenda that one should pursue is to personally discover what the Scriptures actually teach about him. "For many shall come in my name, saying, I am Christ; and shall deceive many" (Matthew 24:5 – KJV). Not only are there false claimants to his Messiahship, but there are those who clearly seek to distort his image for their own diverse reasons. Wisdom and discernment need to characterise the person who desires to arrive at a knowledge of the truth.

"There is some good in this world and it's worth fighting for"

This is a scene from Lord of the Rings, 2nd part *The Two Towers*.[33]

"Though Frodo and Samwise are on the seemingly impossible task of destroying the ring... The difficulties start to arouse doubts in their minds... Looking at the bigger picture makes them feel very small... Samwise: "I know. It's all wrong. By rights we shouldn't even be here. But we are. It's like in the great stories, Mr. Frodo. The ones that really mattered. Full of darkness and danger, they were. And sometimes you didn't want to know the end. Because how could the end be happy? How could the world go back to the way it was when so much bad had happened? But in the end, it's only a passing thing, this shadow. Even darkness must pass. A new day will come.

And when the sun shines it will shine out the clearer. Those were the stories that stayed with you. That meant something, even if you were too small to understand why. But I think, Mr. Frodo, I do understand. I know now. Folk in those stories had lots of chances of turning back, only they didn't. They kept going. Because they were holding on to something."

Frodo: "What are we holding onto, Sam?"[34]

In the quest for the Jewish Yeshua, at times it seems an impossible task, but it too is worthy of holding on to. "There is some good in this world and it's worth fighting for," and that is not only to prove that Yeshua is the Messiah and Lord of all humanity, but equally that he is the Anointed One of Israel. This reality is worth courageously holding onto and fighting for, not with the "arm of the flesh," but it is a battle for the souls of Jewish men and women too.

Paul says what we are truly battling against:

Ephesians 6:12 (NIV), [12] "For our struggle is not against flesh and blood, but against the rulers, against the authorities, against the powers of this dark world and against the spiritual forces of evil in the heavenly realms."

We need to identify that the real enemy is no human agency or being, but it is a spiritual foe with the satanic realm opposing all those who seek to propagate the true gospel of salvation. The Jewish people have faced this opposition since its inception as a nation, and the battle continues until this day with every attempt to deny the truth to both Israel and humankind.

Even the Apostle Peter, having made the acclamation that Yeshua is God's Anointed, in the very next breath became a channel for Satan when he tried to dissuade Yeshua from offering himself as the atoning sacrifice. Yeshua rebuked him sternly, "Get behind me Satan!"

The Ring of Power from Lord of the Rings

9 — In search of the Jesus of history: More on the "Jesus Quest"

A major issue that confronts all who desire to explore the divisions between Judaism and Christianity is the concern about the veracity of the historic Jesus. As Susannah Heschel in her study on the work of *Abraham Geiger and the Jewish Jesus* says, the quest of the historical Jesus was a central concern of nineteenth-century Protestant theologians as people like Albert Schweitzer have demonstrated. Yet Schweitzer displayed an ignorance of the terrible problem that arose when Christians discuss the religious life of the historical figure of Jesus.

"He was a Jew, even though Jesus may be viewed as the first and foremost, greatest Christian of all times, but his life and teaching was within the context of Judaism. Though most modern Protestant scholars wanted to either supress or ignore this fact, 'their German-Jewish colleagues delighted in reminding them of it.'"[35]

A double-edged sword

There is a double-edged sword that is used by both Christian and Jewish scholars who attempt to cut Jesus away from his Jewishness on the one side (the Christian), and on the other, his divine nature and person as the Jewish Messiah and Lord (the Jewish side).

This was well illustrated when I attended a lecture in 2010 at the Rank Centre, Wesley College, Cambridge, UK given by Dr. Geza Vermes, Professor Emeritus, Jewish Studies, Oxford University, UK. He spoke on the subject of "Jesus the Jew" to a mixed Jewish – Christian audience. Dr Vermes demonstrated his skill as a theological swordsman by cutting a division between the Jesus of history and the Jesus of faith. It would appear that this was done deliberately and not inadvertently in his dividing the two aspects of Jesus' person and consequently undermining the possibility of anyone having a living faith in this Jesus of Vermes' imagining. For Vermes, Jesus as Messiah and divine Son of God is off-limits to Jews and for that matter, a very dubious choice for Gentiles to make too.

On the question of the historic Jesus, he said that there was little reliable testimony other than those of the eye-witness accounts of the Gospel writers, and these were biased and more in the realm of propaganda. The Josephus' references to Jesus may have been later interpolations and therefore should not be considered reliable. Though Vermes has written a number of books on the subject of "Jesus the Jew," in his lecture he went way beyond anything that he had put in print, clearly using the forum afforded him by The Cambridge Federation to express his most radically destructive ideas about the question of the historical Jesus.

It occurred to me that the thrust of Dr Vermes' talk had the effect of undermining the reliability of the historical records, and the grounds upon which the Messianic faith makes its affirmations and thus placed this faith upon very shaky ground. Consequently, belief in the "Jesus of faith" was equally undermined by what he said. One was led to conclude that Christian belief was therefore based upon a "myth" and not the fact of a real historical Jesus. The New Testament and the numerous Christian writings about him in the early era would equally have to be viewed as untrustworthy. This may then be called "the greatest deception or hoax of all time," if one was to follow Vermes' line of thought to its logical end. Therefore, anyone who takes this approach consequently would make true bridge building between Jesus and Jewish people well-nigh impossible. For Gentiles though, no such prohibition to believe in Jesus exists. Nonetheless, Dr. Vermes' assertions concerning Jesus equally violates the tenets of the Messianic faith. While one may discover something of Jesus' Jewishness from him, however, in the way in which Dr. Vermes has reclaimed Jesus as a Jew, he effectively alienates him from the New Testament assertion that he is the divine Son of God, Messiah of Israel and Saviour of the world.

Just as Dr Vermes has raised the spectre that the Jesus of history and faith have been carefully fabricated by the disciples of Jesus and those who hold to a traditional interpretation of orthodox Christianity, so equally, we in our attempt to discover the Jesus of faith should not look to those who dispute the veracity of the Gospel message. Our search needs to look elsewhere if we desire to personally discover who the Jewish Jesus is. One such advocate of the Messianic faith is Rav Shaul, a Pharisee, who had a personal encounter with the Risen Messiah on the road to Damascus all those years ago: Acts 9:5 (NIV) [5] "Who are you, Lord?" Saul asked. "I am Jesus, whom you are persecuting," he replied.

Paul and the Jews

Rav Shaul, also known as the Apostle Paul, does have a number of things to say to his fellow Jews. In my blog, through Shalom Radio, UK, during the latter part of 2017, I discussed Shaul's heartfelt concerns for Israel, that is his fellow Jews. In the Epistle to the Romans, in chapters 9–11,

Paul elaborates on the most pressing questions that confront Jewish people concerning Yeshua and Messianic belief.[36]

Rabbi Dr Leo Baeck and Prof. Martin Buber have contributed a considerable amount of serious scholarly work on the person and work of Jesus. They both claim him as a significant Jewish luminary who lived and worked within a first century Jewish context. While they differ as to the details of what he is supposed to have done, they both agree that he lived and died as a thoroughly Jewish man. It is their contention that the Apostle Paul then is the one who started a new religion. They held this happened when he turned his focus towards the Gentile world and interpreted the new Messianic faith in a way that was contrary to the tenets of Second and Post-Second Temple Judaism.

Rabbi Beack took particular issue with what he perceived as Paul's antinomian approach towards the law. He expressed equally strong misgivings about the way that Paul interpreted the outworking of this new faith which he contended was a major departure from Post-Second Temple Judaism. For Rabbi Beack, it is unacceptable that Torah observance should be diluted and at times abandoned by Paul and that he encouraged others to also do so. For Prof. Buber, Paul developed a romanticised kind of faith that deviated from the halachic interpretation of the Torah, ignoring the moral ethical principles of how one should live out one's faith.

Both Baeck and Buber invested many years of studying the New Testament with a particular desire to not only explore the Jewishness of Jesus, but they both desired to see a greater understanding between Jews and Christians who share a common heritage. They were particularly concerned to place

Jesus in his original Jewish context and to counter the negative and destructive influence of the de-Judaizing of the Christian faith.

However, despite the fact that Rabbi Baeck and Prof. Buber both had a prolonged exposure to Christianity and the thinking of certain Christian philosophers and theologians of the late nineteenth and early part of the twentieth century, neither of them were able to satisfactorily resolve their difficulties with Pauline theology.

It has been said that 'isms' lead to schisms and their coining this expression 'Paulism', aptly describes their contentions against Paul. If, as is asserted by them, Paul sufficiently deviated from the tenets of post-Second Temple Judaism, then part of the accusation that he started a new religion called Christianity needs to be seriously considered. How great a deviation was Paul responsible for? Was this new faith that Paul instigated sufficiently different from Judaism as practiced during the first two centuries of the common era?

The original context

We must also keep in mind that there was religious pluralism during that period. Judaism as practiced was not a monochrome faith. There were a number of competing sects and expressions of how Jewish people sought to live out their beliefs. These different expressions of Judaism are gleaned from the wealth of literature of that time – Essenes/Qumran Sect, Pharisees and Sadducees, political parties aligned to the different religious sects, such as the Zealots, and the Nazarenes (Christians). Josephus demonstrated that so serious were some of the disagreements between the rival parties that civil unrest and war threated the status quo. Judea was a very turbulent Roman province that exercised its leadership constantly.

During this turbulent period in Jewish history, a minor Jewish sect, called the Nazarenes, was emerging as an added challenge that increasingly demanded attention from not only the Jewish religious authorities and Roman rulers, but also the Jewish population in general. The motley band of disciples that included fishermen, tax collectors, sick people that had been healed, people that had been raised from the dead, women on the fringes of society and even some members of the ruling counsel of the Sanhedrin, together with a number of priests and some former Pharisees, all now claimed allegiance to Jesus of Nazareth. They said, that the *Crucified – God* was now alive. They declared that he is both Lord and Messiah.

The issues raised by Rabbi Baeck and Prof. Buber concerning their view of the Messianic faith have left a number of unresolved issues surrounding both the person of Yeshua, and also the part that Paul played in shaping it.

Many Jewish and some liberal Christian scholars, have asserted that Jesus was true to the tenets of Second Temple Judaism, but it was the Apostle Paul, the apostle to the Gentiles who created a new religion that became known as Christianity. Jesus observed the Torah's teaching, though at times he challenged some of the Pharisaic dictums, while Paul abandoned the Law completely by his rejection of it. His reason for this was to allow the Gentile believers the ability to follow Christ without first becoming Jews.

10 — In Paul's defence

ROMANS 3:4:
HEAVEN FORBID! GOD WOULD BE TRUE EVEN IF EVERYONE WERE A LIAR! - AS THE TANAKH SAYS, "SO THAT YOU, GOD, MAY BE PROVED RIGHT IN YOUR WORDS AND WIN THE VERDICT WHEN YOU ARE PUT ON TRIAL." (CJB)

In this chapter I explore what Paul says in his own defence against those who hold him responsible for the separation of Judaism and Christianity. I wish also to more fully explore the apostle's heart-cry for Israel, his fellow Jews, his 'kinsfolk according to the flesh'.

Torah or Law

The terms 'Torah' and 'Law' convey various things in both the Jewish and Christian theological worlds. It is important to clarify these two expressions before considering the misgivings that Leo Baeck and Martin Buber express concerning the theological outlook of the Apostle Paul.

The term 'Torah' has a broad and multifaceted meaning and may be applied to the 'Five Books of Moses' (Pentateuch); the Decalogue (10 Commandments); the whole of the Hebrew Scriptures (Tenach); True Teaching; and the Word of the LORD.

While 'Law' in the New Testament, has quite a different meaning derived from the Greek term 'nomos,' it is primarily meant to mean laws or dictums and carries a legal implication. An example in our modern context is that if one were to exceed the speed limit, one is considered guilty of breaking the traffic code and can therefore expect to be punished accordingly.

However, the Greek translation of the of the Hebrew Bible, known as the Septuagint – LXX, translates 'Torah' as 'nomos.' This is the word used in the Greek New Testament for 'Torah' and it is translated into English as Law/law .The narrow New Testament interpretation of 'law' consequently has created numerous and complex problems for both Jewish and Christian theologians. At times they speak at cross purposes and it is particularly so when dealing with Pauline theology. Specifically, its significance is felt in how 'faith' and 'works' are understood. The role of Jesus as asserted by Paul, is affected in the way he is understood and interpreted.

Burning issues

These are just some of the burning issues of contention, that Rabbi Leo Beack, and Prof. Martin Buber have with the Apostle Paul's theological perspective. They particularly cite Paul's letters to the Romans and Galatians. They partly based their arguments upon what they call 'faulty scriptural or biased translations of certain texts' in Romans and Galatians. This factor contributed to Baeck and Buber in their view of what Paul said.

Is Paul 'the bad boy'?

So, is Paul the 'bad boy' of early Jewish-Christian history? Should the blame for the cleavage that occurred between post-Second Temple Judaism and the emergent Messianic faith be squarely laid at his door?

An equally important question to ask is whether Paul tore up the contract/covenant that God had established with the Jewish people and rewrote it in his endeavour to include Gentiles in the New Covenant faith community? Also was he inconsistent and contrary with Jesus' expressed desire that he had not come to abolish or destroy the law, but to fulfil it?

There is clearly a perception difficulty between Baeck and Buber over Paul's point of view. This is foremost in the arguments against Pauline theology that they put forward.

The centre-piece of Pauline theological thinking concerning the Jewish people and their place in the divine plan are in his complex discussion in Romans chapters 9-11. From the outset, it is important to keep in mind that when dealing with these texts from Romans 9–11, though a major hiatus has occurred concerning the question of the Gospel and the relationship between Yeshua (Jesus) and Israel/the Jewish people, they are inseparable. It is Paul's contention that this rupture between them will ultimately be healed.

Israel's election

The Jews are God's special people, or "chosen people." Despite their stubbornness and, at times, rebellious attitude, this unique relationship with God will never change. The promised gospel of the Messiah's advent, foretold in the Hebrew Scriptures, and its message become explicit in the words, 'both for the Jew first and for the Greek (Gentiles) later' (cf. Romans 2.9-10).

It is plain that when thinking of God's faithfulness, the question of Jewish involvement cannot be ignored or glossed over. Though there are numerous texts in Galatians and Romans, it became incumbent upon Paul to discuss this subject at some length in Romans chapters 9–11.

In Romans Paul wrote to the believers concerning their new life in the Messiah. Though many Christian theologians hold that Romans is Paul's major treaties on 'justification by faith,' an equally important theme that runs throughout the letter is the relationship between Jews and Gentiles and their standing before God. There are numerous texts that highlight this (see Romans 1:6-8; 2:12; 2:9-10; 2:14; 2:27; 3:9; 3:30; 4:9; 11:14).

The congregation in Rome was made up of Jews and Gentiles and Paul wanted to help establish their faith and clarify a number of issues that were causing confusion and needed clearing up.

The darkest hour

The darkest hour had dawned with Israel's failure to embrace Yeshua as Messiah and Lord. Because of this rejection of Yeshua by the Judaean Temple leadership, centred around the High Priest and his ruling council, the Jewish believers were being persecuted. Saul/Paul, prior to his enlightenment, was an active persecutor of the believers:

Acts 9:1-2 (NRSV), "[1] Meanwhile Saul, still breathing threats and murder against the disciples of the Lord, went to the high priest [2] and asked him for letters to the synagogues at

Damascus, so that if he found any who belonged to the Way, men or women, he might bring them bound to Jerusalem."

What are the consequences for Judaism that had chosen another path other than acknowledging Yeshua as Messiah and Lord? What hope is left for the Jewish people? However, painful as it is, all hope is not lost. A breakdown in the relationship between Israel and her God is not final nor irrevocable.

In Romans 9, Paul outlines some of his thinking about their destiny:

Romans 9 (NRSV), [1] "I am speaking the truth in Christ – I am not lying; my conscience confirms it by the Holy Spirit – [2] I have great sorrow and unceasing anguish in my heart. [3] For I could wish that I myself were accursed and cut off from Christ for the sake of my own people, my kindred according to the flesh. [4] They are Israelites, and to them belong the adoption, the glory, the covenants, the giving of the law, the worship, and the promises; [5] to them belong the patriarchs, and from them, according to the flesh, comes the Messiah, who is over all, God blessed forever. Amen." Paul's sigh over their fall is a sign of deep personal anguish, yet the fall is not so absolute as to imply a nullification of God's purpose for Israel.

The promises made to Israel, though they have been severely disrupted, do not mean that there is no way back or no hope of restoration. Divine sovereignty in the Hebrew Scriptures makes it clear that God is not unjust when he selects one person or group to fulfil his plan and purpose. One may be chosen for a high purpose, while another for a lowly one.

God's sovereignty allows him to respond to human initiative as he chooses: "Humankind proposes, God disposes!"

Therefore, in the Jewish response to Yeshua, God fulfils his purpose. While a hardening came upon Israel in part it was so that the Gentiles may be included in the family of God. The natural branches were cut off the olive tree and the wild ones were grafted in! (See Romans 11.11-24)

However, both Jews and Gentiles are personally held accountable for their response to God's initiative in his plan of salvation. Examples of God's choice are displayed when he chose Israel and not Edom; Moses to display his mercy and Pharaoh his anger; he will select some Jews and some Gentiles to be members of his Messianic Kingdom.

Let us be clear, while God chooses some to show his favour, it does not imply therefore he has chosen to damn some. Paul does not say this here in Romans 9. Nothing is said about eternal life or death. God uses his judgment and compassionate mercy at the same time as he sees fit to fulfil his divine plan. God is not unjust for he is both righteous and a just judge and always responds towards humanity with fairness.

Many people question Israel's future?

Many people question Israel's future. This is particularly those who hold to a supersessionist and the replacement theological position concerning Israel and the concept of a chosen people. As far as they are concerned the Jewish people have fulfilled their divine calling by bringing Christ into the world and they are no longer chosen any more than anyone else is. There is no special or particular plan for them. They have become just like all the other nations and they must find their place in the same way that others do. They are not excluded from God's plan of salvation, but no special promises apply to them. This type of argument flies in the face of the New Testament teaching by Yeshua, his disciples and particularly the Apostle Paul who, in Romans 9–11, has devoted a considerable amount of his writing in which he painstakingly has argued for the continued position of divine favour. While this showing of God's favour to the Jewish people does not imply that they have another way to be included in God's household – the olive tree motif is used to illustrate the point that Paul has made.

Both the wild and natural branches serve to make up a healthy olive tree. Both are included and the Jewish people will once more find their place in God's olive tree: Romans 11:24, "For if thou wert cut out of the olive tree which is wild by nature, and wert grafted contrary to nature into a good olive tree: how much more shall these, which be the natural branches, be grafted into their own olive tree?" (KJV)

The promises of God are trustworthy and will not fail, whatever people may think or say.

Supersessionist and Replacement theology

Supersessionist and Replacement theological thinking has plagued the church from early times and it has helped to drive the Jewish people even further away from the gospel message. This thinking holds to the lie that God has finished with Israel as a people of his covenant. Why on earth then should Jewish people want anything to do with those who not only claim that Israel is rejected, but have also plundered them of their scriptures, the TENACH – Hebrew Bible. They call it the Old Testament which to Jewish people is both demeaning and helps to relegate it to a secondary position. This helped develop a heretical Marcionite rejection of the Hebrew Scriptures entirely.

In the process the Messianic faith has been de-Judaized and, in its place, a Hellenised faith stands. They have forcibly sought to convert Jews to a Christianity that despises and declares itself as having replaced Judaism. The Jews are no longer viewed as the chosen people, but the rejected people. Not only has the church taken all the blessing promised to Israel, but they have conveniently left the curses for hapless Israel. Truly this is a travesty and tragedy, and this is one of the reasons that we need to engage in the battle to restore Israel to its rightful place in the plan of God.

∗

Warning!

DANGER

Those who advocate Replacement theology are in great danger spiritually of distorting the truth

Graphic created by Roni Mechanic ©

11 — The human response:

What are we to say then about the purposes of God? What is the calling that he has placed upon you? Are you called to lead or follow? Are you a Jew or a Gentile? Are you male or female? Most importantly, how may you be included in Messiah Yeshua?

The choice is up to each individual to respond to the light and grace of God that they have received.

This desire and prayer are the heart of the matter that rests very heavily upon Paul as he considers the plight of Israel.

"My heart's desire and prayer to God for them is that they may be saved," (Romans 10.1b)

A heart ablaze or a heart moved by compassion, is a powerful image that, like the sun though burning with intense heat, yet it is not consumed. So, this passion for the Jewish people that the great emissary of the faith expresses in this section of his letter to the Romans in chapter 10 is something that is of deep concern to him and his passion for Israel cannot be extinguished.

What does it mean to be saved?

In the Introduction to the Jewish New Testament, translated by Dr David Stern in 1979, he asks the question "Why the Jewish New Testament?"[37]

He continues, to answer the question, "Why the Jewish New Testament is different from all other New Testaments...

because [it] expresses its original and essential Jewishness. Nearly all other English translations of the New Testament – and there literally hundreds – present its message in a Gentile-Christian linguistic, cultural and theological framework."[38] (Stern, 1979:ix)

What Dr Stern has said about the English versions of the New Testament, can equally be applied to the German, French, Dutch, Spanish, Italian, Afrikaans and other translations of the New Testament. For the reader who is unfamiliar with biblical jargon, let me clarify the term "salvation." It is one of the many Hebrew words used to signify God's act in redeeming or delivering humankind.

The way that biblical terminology is used and how they translate both Hebrew and Greek words impact not only upon our discussion on the subject of salvation but can equally be applied to numerous other Scriptural texts in the New Testament. Because we are facing the challenge posed by Dr Baeck, Prof Buber and other Jewish philosophers and theologians, the type of theological mind-set and bias is equally important when dealing with New Testament texts.

"Yasa" [yasha] means variously, "to save, help in distress, rescue, deliver, set free." It appears most frequently in the Hebrew Scriptures and, commonly, this deliverance given in the Hebrew Scriptures speaks in a material sense in nature, though there are important exceptions. In contrast, the employment of "soteria" (Greek) in the New Testament, though it may include material preservation, usually signifies deliverance with special spiritual significance. In addition to the notion of deliverance, the Bible also uses salvation to denote health, well-being, and healing.

One might say that salvation is the overriding theme of the entire Bible. But since it is a multidimensional theme with a wide range of meaning, simple definitions are impossible. The biblical writers speak of "salvation" as a reality with both a spiritual and physical dimension. It has individual and communal aspects to it, with an objective and subjective application, as well as an eternal and historical dimension. Since the biblical writers' view of salvation has an historical reality, the temporal dimensions of past, present, and future further intensify and deepen the concept.

Salvation is a process with a beginning and an end. We are being saved or we are being delivered.

As has been previously stated, salvation involves both human freedom and divine election. We are given freedom to serve God, but God chooses who will serve him. This is a biblical tension truth or, some may say, a paradox?

The Bible constantly speaks about "salvation" in the context of concrete relationships between humans and God. It not only includes personal salvation, but it also has a redemptive concern for the world in which we live. God is the main initiator throughout the process in the example of the deliverance of Noah and his family through to the great multitude that shouts, "Salvation belongs to our God, who sits on the throne, and to the Lamb!" (Rev 7:10).

In Judaism, salvation from sin, though not a dominant concern, is by no means absent especially in the prophets. As much as he is concerned for Israel's national restoration, Ezekiel stresses the need for salvation from uncleanness, iniquity and idolatry (Ezekiel 36:22-32). Here salvation involves the gift of a new heart of flesh and new spirit which will finally empower his people to keep the commandments, after which comes habitation in the land.

In this passage too, we encounter a common refrain – such salvation, when it comes, will be neither for the sake of Israel nor her deeds, but for God and his glory. Isaiah tells of a salvation still on the way which will be achieved through the vicarious suffering of the Servant of the LORD (chap. 53) who bears the sin of many. This salvation will last forever. (51:6) The prophet Jeremiah in his famous chapter (31:31f) also speaks of a new covenant which is promised:

"The days are surely coming says the LORD when I will make a new covenant with the House of Israel and the House of Jacob. It will not be like the covenant that I made with their ancestors, when I took them by the hand to bring them out of the Land of Egypt, a covenant that they broke though I was their husband, says the LORD. But this is the covenant that I will make with the House of Israel after those days says, the LORD. I will put my law within them, and I will write it on their hearts, and I will be their God, and they shall be my people" (Jer. 31:31-33).

We should note that each of the prophetic writers expresses a similar notion that God is going to bring about a radical change, establishing a new covenant with the house of Israel.

The anticipated salvation of the prophetic writings manifests a tension similar to that which pervades the New Testament. While salvation is a *fait accompli*, God saved Israel from slavery in Egypt into a covenant relationship with himself. Israel still awaits God's salvation. God has saved Israel in the past and, therefore, God can be expected to deliver her in the future. Whatever else salvation may be from a biblical perspective, its dimensions of "settled past" and "anticipated future" show it in its widest scope to be an elongated reality covering the entire trajectory of history. The "not yet, already" tension is discussed in numerous theological works.

George Ladd in his book *The Presence of the Future* discusses the issue of the fact that In Christ, the Kingdom is both present and future. Rudolf Otto's influential *The Kingdom of God and the Son of Man* understands the Kingdom of God to be the heavenly realm where God's will is done, the suprahistorical sphere where God rules. Jesus' teaching is grounded in a dualism of earth vs heaven. The heavenly realm is a "wholly other" existence, and Jesus announced the coming of this miraculous supernatural realm.

This event is exclusively God's deed and will mean the breaking off of history and the descent of the heavenly realm to earth. The Kingdom of heaven will come down from above and effect a marvellous transformation of the world. The Lord's Prayer is a petition for the coming of this supernatural, heavenly realm. However, Jesus believed that the Kingdom was already in the process of coming. This he believed because in a vision he had seen Satan overthrown in heaven. (Luke 10:18) Therefore, he knew that God had already achieved victory over Satan and that the Kingdom had already been realised in heaven. A tidal wave of divine victory had been set up by virtue of which the powers of the Kingdom [The Kingdom of God] were already operative on earth. This is what Rudolf Otto means by his oft-quoted statement, "It is not Jesus who brings the kingdom... the kingdom brings him with it."[39]

The future heavenly realm is already breaking into the world through Jesus in the form of the wonderful, supernatural, coercive power operating from above. "The Kingdom is not only the eschatological realm, it is also victorious, coercive power. The eschatological realm of salvation is already breaking into the world as a divine *dynamis* (the state of that which is not yet fully realised as in power or potential). In the future age Jesus will become the heavenly Son of Man; but he is already the agent of the present in-breaking power of the Kingdom."[40]

This recognition has helped recent biblical scholarship to avoid the earlier pitfall of relegating the role of the Hebrew Scriptures to that of mere preparation or precursor for the Gospel. One cannot escape the fact that for the Jews of the Hebrew Scriptures, salvation was not an abstract concept, but a real and present experience. The Psalms are replete with praise for God's salvation which is experienced as joy. (51:12) It is a cup of thanksgiving lifted to God (116:13) and a horn (18:2). Elsewhere salvation is depicted as a torch (Isa. 62:1), a well (Isa.12:3) and a shield (2 Sam 22:36).

Martin Buber had tremendous difficulty with the New Testament declaration that in Jesus the Kingdom of God had come when clearly, all around, one witnesses anything but the universal peace that the dawning of the messianic age is meant to bring. Ladd, Otto, Schweitzer and many other theologians have attempted to explain the apparent contradiction in the Christian declaration that the Kingdom of God has come with the Advent of Jesus.

As an aside – Martin Buber had a personal encounter with both Rudolf Otto and Albert Schweitzer. He found them both the most gracious and loving, accepting people. Buber said of his meeting with Otto that he felt something of the 'numinous' presence of the "holy other," when he was with him.

In Rudolph Otto's book the *Idea of the Holy*, he explains the Presence of God as the 'numinous' or shining brightness of the Holy Other. This 'encounter' that Buber experienced was no doubt something to do with that manifestation of the 'Presence' that he felt.

Albert Schweitzer's openness to the world and his person and life was an inspiration to Buber as well as his peculiar nearness to Israel that was possible for Christians and Christian theologians. In his book *Two Types of Faith*, he recalls with fond memory the many hours of walking that Schweitzer and he enjoyed and which they shared, as it were, heart-to-heart and "through that of the spirit." Buber recalled that Schweitzer wrote of the Apostle Paul that he "has his roots in the Jewish world of thought and not the Greek."[41] Buber recalls that it was through Schweitzer that he was impressed to undertake an in-depth study of Paul, which he subsequently did.

Major stumbling blocks

One of the major stumbling blocks for Jewish people is when they ask the question that if Yeshua was meant to inaugurate the Kingdom of Heaven on earth, "then where is the universal peace that Isaiah spoke of?"

This is not only a dilemma for Jewish people, but many people who desire universal peace and an end to war question the veracity of the claim that Yeshua is the long awaited, Messiah and Prince of Peace spoken of by Isaiah in his declaring his Messianic name as, "Wonderful Councillor, the Mighty God and Prince of Peace":

"For unto us a child is born, unto us a son is given: and the government shall be upon his shoulder: and his name shall be called Wonderful, Counsellor, The mighty God, The everlasting Father, The Prince of Peace." (Isaiah 9:6)

On a recent album by Paul McCartney, Egypt Station (2018), he includes a song called: "People Want Peace!" So, where is that elusive 'peace' that is meant to accompany the Messianic age?

Swords to ploughshares

Swords to ploughshares is a metaphor for the transformation and anticipation that, in the messianic age to come – military weapons and technologies will be converted for peaceful use into useful implements of production in industry and farming tools.

The phrase originates from the Book of Isaiah:

And many people shall go and say, "Come ye, and let us go up to the mountain of the Lord, to the house of the God of Jacob; and He will teach us of His ways, and we will walk in His paths: for out of Zion shall go forth the law, and the word of the Lord from Jerusalem. And He shall judge among the nations and shall rebuke many people: and they shall beat their swords into ploughshares, and their spears into pruning hooks: nation shall not lift up sword against nation, neither shall they learn war anymore." (Isaiah 2:3-4 - KJV)

Yet, in the light of Ladd's thesis that the kingdom of heaven is breaking into this world, this indicates that the establishment of that rule of God is a progressive and gradual realisation. It will face a climax with the Parousia. The Greek παρουσία is an ancient Greek word meaning 'presence', 'arrival', or 'the official visit of the Second-Advent of the Messiah.'

Two Messiahs?

The Jewish understanding of the advent of the Messiah is that there is only one coming and not two. However, there is a tradition that describes the Mashiach as both Messiah Ben Joseph and also Messiah Ben David. The former image of Messiah Ben Joseph is an enigmatic figure.

While Messiah Ben David fulfils the traditional role of the conquering, triumphant deliverer who will restore the Davidic kingdom at the end of the age, Ben Joseph in a considerable measure may be equated to a suffering Messiah.

To cover the main features concerning Ben Joseph

He is despised and rejected by his brothers; betrayed; sold into slavery; reckoned dead by his father; he went down into a forced exile in Egypt; was falsely accused and imprisoned; languished in prison for a long time; brought forth from the prison; restored and raised to second in command over all of Egypt. Then he revealed himself to his brothers who wept when they recognised him and, finally, he was revealed to his aged father who had lost all hope of finding his son alive.

He is viewed as one returned from the dead

There are stark similarities to that of Yeshua as the "Suffering Servant," who was despised and rejected by the house of his brothers, i.e. fellow Jews; was handed over to the Romans who put him to death by crucifixion; but God raised him up from the dead; he appeared to his followers (over 500); and he ascended into heaven and now he sits at the right had of Majesty on High; He will return to the earth and set up his kingdom; and all will recognise him. The challenge that Judaism has yet to face is how to reconcile these two images of the Messiah? Not two Messiahs, but one person who has a two-fold role to fulfil. The Suffering Servant motif has already been fulfilled at his first advent, while the second part of his purpose as the Messiah King is yet to happen at the Parousia (Second Coming/Second Advent).

It is only through divine revelation that the veil of blindness will be removed from Jewish perception. Then they shall look upon him who they have pierced. Their tears of shame and guilt will turn to shouts of joy when they not only recognise him but receive him as Messiah and Lord.

Zechariah 12:10 KJV, "And I will pour upon the house of David, and upon the inhabitants of Jerusalem, the spirit of grace and of supplications: and they shall look upon me whom they have pierced, and they shall mourn for him, as one mourneth for his only son, and shall be in bitterness for him, as one that is in bitterness for his firstborn."

This is part of my story and longing for my fellow Jews and this is my prayer that they will also make the same discovery that I and a growing number of other Jewish people are making.

Nearly saved

The parable of the rich young ruler well illustrates the case of someone who was very near the Kingdom of Heaven: Luke 18:18-23 (KJV) [18] "And a certain ruler asked him, saying, Good Master, what shall I do to inherit eternal life? [19] And Jesus said unto him, Why callest thou me good? none is good, save one, that is, God. [20] Thou knowest the commandments, Do not commit adultery, Do not kill, Do not steal, Do not bear false witness, Honour thy father and thy mother. [21] And he said, All these have I kept from my youth up. [22] Now when Jesus heard these things, he said unto him, Yet lackest thou one thing: sell all that thou hast, and distribute unto the poor, and thou shalt have treasure in heaven: and come, follow me. [23] And when he heard this, he was very sorrowful: for he was very rich."

Though this is a parable it describes a very real-life choice with which this rich young man was confronted. While it would appear that his wealth was the blockage to him following Yeshua, there are many reasons that folk when confronted with the challenge of following Yeshua, equally pull back.

There are a number of prominent Jewish people who have written about their nearly becoming a disciple of Yeshua. Franz Rosenzweig and Will Herberg are two such twentieth century Jewish scholars that had seriously considered becoming believers but pulled away, partly under the influence of Reinhold Niebuhr with whom they had both been in correspondence. Niebuhr had dissuaded them due to his Dual-covenant theology that held that Judaism, together with Christianity, were on an equal footing and that while Gentiles needed to be converted, no such requirement should be required of Jews who already were included in a covenant relationship with God.

Rabbi Blue, the Oxford Reform rabbi and radio personality that regularly spoke on *Thought for the Day* on BBC Radio 4, had an encounter with the 'holy other' or had a sense of the numinous while he was a student at Oxford University when he was present at a Quaker meeting. He called it a mystical experience and while he contemplated becoming a follower of Yeshua, instead he decided to train to become a Jewish Reform rabbi. Blue said that he had a life-long fascination with Christianity but never became a convinced follower of Yeshua.

Someone may say "I too could become of follower of Yeshua" but for whatever reasons, they hold back and are unable to make that all-important decision to make a lasting commitment to become a disciple of Yeshua HaMashiach. That all-important step is costly and should not be undertaken half-heartedly, for one may well face opposition, rejection and sometimes open hostility and persecution.

Personally challenged

Though I have faced many challenges, I have no regrets. It is the best thing that I have ever done in my life as a Jewish person to put my faith in Yeshua the Messiah. I have come to love and know God, his Torah and his Messiah, Yeshua. I am still learning and discovering the richness of his free unmerited gift of grace which he freely gives to all who turn to him.

Yeshua warned his followers that just as he was rejected, so those who follow him can equally anticipate opposition and rejection. Before I took the step to embrace Yeshua as Messiah and Lord, I read a book called: *They Looked for a City*, by Lydia Buksbazen.[42] This book describes the epic story of a Jewish family who, having embraced Yeshua, were rejected and persecuted by their fellow Jews for having become believers. I knew that if I took the step it would be costly.

They Looked for a City

Many years ago, I heard Lydia Buksbazen speak at a meeting of the British Messianic Jewish Alliance in London, UK. She related something of the epic journey of her family. She gave an account of her Eastern European Jewish family from Poland, which is a bitter, yet triumphant story of survival despite being confronted by the Russian Cossacks who violently attacked Jewish people in a market town.

"Their lives weave a tale of betrayal and separation, confusion and desperation, failure and success. Caught in the maelstrom of war, their little family is torn apart by a devastating series of events, producing a heart-breaking situation with no apparent solution. Yet in the midst of international chaos and conflict, God performs a miracle you'll never forget." (back cover of *They Looked for a City*, Friends of Israel Gospel Ministry, NY, USA, 1955)

This book is an amazing account of the Buksbazen family's great courage and fortitude in the face of adversity. Though my life's journey was very different to theirs, nonetheless, I too, have faced many challenges but it was after due consideration that I made my decision. This book helped me to count the cost of what it might mean to embrace and follow Yeshua as Messiah and Lord.

Luke 14 [28] "For which of you, intending to build a tower, does not first sit down and estimate the cost, to see whether he has enough to complete it? [29] Otherwise, when he has laid a foundation and is not able to finish, all who see it will begin to ridicule him, [30] saying, 'This fellow began to build and was not able to finish.'" (NRSV).

Counting the cost is very important if one's commitment is to be a lasting one, for opposition will have to be faced and turning back is perilous spiritually.

Belief, confession and follow through

Becoming a believer is more than just having a set of beliefs. The next step that needs to take place to make it happen is a verbal confession of faith based on an inner conviction that includes an acknowledgement that Yeshua is Lord, and that God has raised him from the dead.

Romans 10:9, "That if you confess with your lips and believe in your heart that Yeshua is Lord and that God has raised him from the dead, then you will be saved (delivered)." (CJB)

The follow-through on that initial decision is as important as the verbal confession. Without nurture and nourishment, the seeds of faith will shrivel up and die.

I am exceedingly grateful to those who nurtured me along the road in my Messianic walk. Pastoral guidance and support are vital components in the discipleship process and those who are able to offer this to the young in the faith fulfil a most important role.

Paul speaks in Ephesians 4 of the ministry gifts:

[11] "Furthermore, he gave some people as emissaries, some as prophets, some as proclaimers of the Good News, and some as shepherds and teachers. [12] Their task is to equip God's people for the work of service that builds the body of the Messiah, [13] until we all arrive at the unity implied by trusting and knowing the Son of God, at full manhood, at the standard of maturity set by the Messiah's perfection." (CJB)

No-one would dream of giving birth to a baby and abandoning it. So too, spiritual children equally need to be nurtured and spiritually fed.

1 Peter 2 [2] "As newborn babes, desire the sincere milk of the word, that ye may grow thereby." (KJV) Spiritual growth is a process and it takes its time until one grows to maturity.

1 Corinthians 13:11 (NRSV),
[11] When I was a child, I spoke like a child, I thought like a child, I reasoned like a child; when I became an adult, I put an end to childish ways.

Hebrews 6:1-3 (CJB)
[1] Therefore, leaving behind the initial lessons about the Messiah, let us go on to maturity, not laying again the foundation of turning from works that lead to death, trusting God, [2] and instruction about washings [baptisms], s'mikhah [laying on of hands], the resurrection of the dead and eternal punishment. [3] And, God willing, this is what we will do.

Milk is to be followed by solid food and spiritually speaking, that implies that one needs to not only be nurtured, but also there will come a time when the disciple becomes one who disciples others.

Discipleship is a vital part of being established in the faith, and this is true not only for new believers, but even for those who have been believers for a number of years. Just as in the natural world, so too in the spiritual life, the metaphors of 'milk' for infants and 'meat' (solid food) for grownups, must be stressed if spiritual life is to not only be sustained, but also for spiritual growth is to continue.

God Speaks Through the Holy Scriptures

12 — A verbal confession

Returning to Paul in Romans, we notice he enjoined confession with the mouth that "Yeshua is Lord" and belief that God raised him from the dead. (Rom 10:8-9) The writer of Hebrews suggests that the hearing of the gospel is of no value unless combined with faith (4:1). And this is repeated in James' epistle, where he says, that if you claim to have faith and you do not have works, your faith is dead and meaningless. Demonstrate your faith by the things that you do.[43]

According to Paul two things initially need to happen to be saved:
Romans 10 [9] that if you acknowledge publicly with your mouth that Yeshua is Lord and trust in your heart that God raised him from the dead, you will be delivered. [10] For with the heart one goes on trusting and thus continues toward righteousness, while with the mouth one keeps on making public acknowledgement and thus continues toward deliverance. (CJB)

An outward verbal confession and an inward belief that Yeshua is Lord and that God has raised him from the dead, these are the two vital components that are required to begin your journey into life.

The fact that one acknowledges Yeshua as Lord involves submitting one's life to the leadership of the Messiah and accepting his divine authority with the full implications of that new reality as a member of his Messianic Kingdom. There are important consequences that will begin to transpire in one's life and then one will need to answer the question:

"How shall we then live? Judaism speaks about this as Halacha [how shall we walk?]. How do we interpret the new Messianic faith and live it out in our daily lives?"

There are moral and ethical implications of seeking to follow the Messiah and this should deeply impact upon how we live. As we saw in the example of Zacchaeus, his thieving and self-centred lifestyle were instantly transformed by his encounter with Yeshua. He repaid those whom he had defrauded double and also gave away half his wealth to the poor. John the Baptiser and Yeshua both have harsh words for those who make a profession of faith and whose lives are not transformed by God's life-giving Spirit.

The second part of one's confession is a belief in the resurrection of Yeshua. Paul says that if Yeshua did not rise from the dead, we are the most miserable of all folk and our faith is futile. (see 1 Corinthians 15) This is because not only are we believing a lie, but we are propagating a falsehood and we are surely self-deceived and deceiving others too.

Without the resurrection factor the Messianic house falls down and we are all indeed very lost! But Messiah has been raised and the tomb is empty.

In our studies in Romans 9–11 we consider the weighty question as to whether God has rejected the Jewish people? Many who hold to this viewpoint assert that this is due to their failure to embrace Jesus/Yeshua as Messiah and Lord?

Romans 10 (NRSV), [1] "Brothers and sisters, my heart's desire and prayer to God for them is that they may be saved. [2] I can testify that they have a zeal for God, but it is not enlightened. ³ For, being ignorant of the righteousness that comes from God, and seeking to establish their own, they have not submitted to God's righteousness. ⁴ For Christ is the end of the law so that there may be righteousness for everyone who believes."

Romans 10 (CJB), ¹"Brothers [and sisters], my heart's deepest desire and my prayer to God for Isra'el is for their salvation; ² for I can testify to their zeal for God. But it is not based on correct understanding; ³ for, since they are unaware of God's way of making people righteous and instead seek to set up their own, they have not submitted themselves to God's way of making people righteous. ⁴ For the goal at which the Torah aims is the Messiah, who offers righteousness to everyone who trusts."

These two translations not only bring out different nuances and theologically significant differences to the meaning of the text but, more seriously, the way that Western Christians have translated the Scriptures in certain places have far reaching implications for the Jewish reader.

The translation of verse 4 in the NRSV displays a distinctively Gentile Christian emphasis and bias to its meaning, for by saying that Christ (Messiah) is the 'end of the law,' is one of the reasons that Baeck and Buber have a serious problem with what they perceive Paul is saying. However, if 'the goal at which Torah aims is the Messiah,' Paul had something quite different in mind and Yeshua does not nullify the Law/Torah but is in fact the aim or goal of it.

Romans 10.4:
[German:] ⁴ "Denn Christus ist des Gesetzes Ende; wer an den glaubt, der ist gerecht."

[English:] ⁴ "For Christ is at the end of the law; he who believes in him is just."

The German verse has the identical theological bias, in which Christ is declared to be at the end of the law. We should note that most English versions translate this verse as "the end of the law" with only a few exceptions:

The New International Version, ⁴ "Christ is the "culmination of the law" so that there may be righteousness for everyone who believes."

In the Aramaic Bible in Plain English: ⁴ "The Messiah is 'the consummation of The Written Law' for righteousness to everyone who believes."

And in The Complete Jewish Bible: ⁴ For "the goal at which the Torah aims is the Messiah, who offers righteousness to everyone who trusts." "It therefore follows, Shaul says, that a person who trusts in God which the Torah itself requires, precisely he [she] has this trust which founds the ground of all obedience to the Torah (1.5), understands and responds to the Gospel by also trusting in God's Messiah Yeshua."[44]

As Dr. Stern says, "An error made here by all major English NT translations of this text is the rendering of the Greek word, 'telos' as "end" not "goal." This implies the termination of the Torah, which is often understood to mean that the law (nomos - Greek) has been abolished."[45]

The Church has been characterised for over two millennia by a serious anti-Judaism bias. At times it was done intentionally and at other times through ignorance and bad theology. As a consequence, this has resulted in those involved in translating the Scriptures into German or English giving expression to their theological predisposition and outlook.

A multitude of consequences that arise:

Following that line of thought many will hold that God is finished with the Jews, because they have fulfilled their divinely appointed role to produce the Messiah – Jesus Christ. Also, because of Israel's failure at not recognising Jesus as their Messiah and Lord, God has rejected them. The Law has been superseded and abolished with the revelation of the grace of God given through Christ. Salvation is not through earning any merit by keeping the Law, but all that is needed is to trust in Jesus.

The church is the new Israel and old Israel has been rejected. There are no longer any abiding covenants that Israel can claim as her own, apart from Christ. The land of Israel is only of historic, and archaeological interest. The concept of the *chosen people* is a vanity that Jewish people cling to, and it is like a relic of the past and has no further significance whatsoever. Equally, the Land of Israel does not belong to the Jews any longer and to claim it as their own is a lie because they have stolen it from the Arabs who lived there before the Jews began to occupy it in the nineteenth century. The Holy Scriptures belong to the Christian church which has inherited both Old and New Testaments. Paul's heart's desire for the salvation of Israel in Romans 9–11 is not for the Jews but for the church who are the new Israel.
Shocked

You may be shocked by such an interpretation of the consequence of two thousand year of an anti-Judaism bias. It is my intention to shock you and give you a sense of outrage at such a flagrant denial of the Jewish people's claim to anything other than divine wrath and judgment. I have done this with the deliberate intention to induce you to reconsider the outcome of bad theology and where it leads.

Contrary to holding to an anti-Judaism bias, those who love God and hold to his promises need equally to revisit their theological interpretation instead of perpetuating these negative attitudes toward Israel and the Jewish people. Theological and spiritual renewal needs to take place. Bad theology about Israel and the Jews needs to be replaced with sound biblical interpretation and insight. Instead of being wall and barrier builders, we need to become bridge builders. Let us strive to build bridges of hope and love to enable Jewish people to rediscover their true biblical heritage as sons and daughters of the living God.

Jewish believers are not immune from holding negative theological attitudes towards Judaism, and this is particularly the case when their theological formation has taken place under the tutelage of teachers who hold to negative stereotypes and an anti-Judaism bias.

Whatever one's background, we all need to strive for a good theological understanding and approach to Judaism and the Jewish heritage and background to our common faith. "You worship what you do not know; we worship what we know, for salvation is from the Jews" (John 4:22 – ESV).

13 — The New Testament

A New Testament perspective will aid our understanding of the transition that took place with the advent of Yeshua and the claims that are made concerning his true identity. He clearly challenged the status quo of his day and the impact of his coming continues to be a challenge to Judaism. Uncomfortable as this fact may be, it needs to be reckoned with.

The name Immanuel, "God with us," signifies momentous progress in the history of salvation. Matthew records the occasion when the angel told Joseph that Mary's child was conceived of the Holy Spirit and that he is "to give him the name Yeshua/Jesus, because he will save his people from their sins" (see Matt. 1:21-23). 'Jesus' is the name from the Hebrew name Yeshua/Joshua and means salvation. The purpose for the Son of Man's coming is to seek out and save the lost. (Luke 19:10) The New Testament continues the Hebrew Scripture's affirmation that salvation belongs to God alone, but with greater specificity. Now it is God's presence in and through the man Yeshua that proves decisive.

In Yeshua's teaching, salvation is linked to the advance of God's kingdom, which finds expression in Yeshua's own person. The advent of God's kingdom became a synonym for salvation. Yeshua deepens the Hebrew Scripture's conviction that salvation belongs to God for it is in his kingdom that the reality of God reigns sovereign. Yeshua understood himself to be that harbinger of God's kingdom; and this is evident in the claim following his synagogue reading, "Today this scripture is fulfilled in your hearing" (Luke 4:21 - NIV). Salvation belongs to those who follow

Yeshua, who is the embodiment of God's kingdom. Salvation is described as the mystery of God that is now revealed (Eph. 3:9; 6:19); a plan conceived before the foundations of the world (Eph. 1:3-14); "The Light for the revelation of the Gentiles and The Glory to your people Israel" (Luke 2:30-32 - Aramaic Bible in Plain English). A transition from death to life takes place (John 5:24). It is a message especially for sinners (Mark 2:17), and is a gift of grace through faith which is not achieved through any human effort (Eph. 2:8-9).

In response to Nicodemus's question about how one can be "born anew," Yeshua says that salvation is a spiritual birth, "a birth from above," without which one cannot enter the kingdom of heaven (John 3:1-11). Salvation means death to and freedom from sin (Rom. 6). It is a new perspective that transcends the human point of view and is a participation in a new creation (Rom. 5:16-17). It is an achievement of peace with God (Rom 5:1). Through salvation a new life as adopted children of God is gained (Gal 4:4). Salvation encompasses both the physical and spiritual dimensions of life, having relevance for the whole human person. On the physical side, entrance into the kingdom requires attention to earthly needs, especially those for the poor. Yeshua demands that a wealthy man give his riches to help the poor (Mark 10:17-22). The Socio-economic implications of the message are far reaching and both life-changing and life-challenging.

We witness the salvation that came to Zacchaeus' house inspiring him to give half his possessions to the poor. (Luke 19:8-10) Care for the poor was a regular function of the earliest believing communities. (Acts 9:36; Acts 10:4; Acts 10:31; 24:17; Gal 2:10; James 2:1-7)

For Yeshua the physical and spiritual dimensions are held very closely together. Forgiveness of sins and physical healing frequently coexist, as in the healing of the paralytic (Mark 2:1-12). Other healings done in Yeshua' name call attention to the connection of body, mind and spirit (Acts 3:16; 4:7-12). In these examples, salvation means not only forgiveness of sin but alleviation of its effects.[46]

While Salvation's history [from the German: heilsgeschichte] is an interpretation of history emphasising God's saving acts and viewing Jesus Christ as central in redemption. It reaches a climax in the context of Judaism of the Second Temple era, and we must remember that this is where the Messianic manifestation was realised.

To quote Rabbi Leo Baeck, in his desire to rescue Jesus for Judaism, he shows that the kernel of Jesus' teaching lies in its fidelity to the essence of Judaism and only there.

"In all of his traits, Jesus is through and through a genuinely Jewish character. Such a man as he could only grow up on the soil of Judaism, only there and nowhere else. Jesus is a genuine Jewish personality; all of his striving and acting, his bearing and feeling, his speech and his silence, all of it bears the Jewish stamp, the imprint of… the best that was found in Judaism. Indeed, at that time [prior to the gifts Judaism bestowed on the church] this was at best found only in Judaism… From no other people could such a man as he have arisen, and in no other people could a man such he have been able to work; and in no other people would he have found the apostles who believed in him."[47]

However, the universality of the message of salvation could not be contained within the bounds of Second Temple Judaism for it was God's intention, as predicted through the Jewish prophets and Jesus himself, that the message must also extend beyond the parameters of national Jewish identity. On at least one occasion, Jesus corrects (or at least sidesteps) national expectations concerning the establishing of the Kingdom of God. Once in response to the disciples' question (Acts 1:6-8) and once on the Emmaus road. (Luke 24:25-26). Since Jesus' death was for all people (John 11:51), repentance and forgiveness of sins were to be proclaimed to all nations. (Luke 24:47). This gospel, says Paul, was given in advance in the form of God's promise to bless all the nations through Abraham (Galatians 3:8).

The objective basis and means of salvation is God's sovereign and gracious choice to be "God with us" in the person of Yeshua the Messiah, who is described as both the author and mediator of salvation. (Heb. 2:10; 7:25) But the movement of Jesus' life goes through the cross and resurrection. It is therefore Messiah crucified that is of central importance for salvation (1 Cor. 1:23), for "Jesus died for our sins according to the Scriptures" (1 Cor.15:3) and was handed to death for our trespasses. (Rom 4:25) What Jesus did in our name he also did in our place, giving "his life as a ransom for many" (Matt 20:28). And if Jesus demonstrated his love by dying when we were still sinners, how much more shall we now be saved by his life? (Rom 5:8-10) So critical is the resurrection to the future hope of salvation that "If Jesus has not been raised, your faith is futile; you are still in your sins" (1 Cor. 15:17).

14 — "Has God rejected His people?"

The question of Judaism's standing as a God-given faith is without question, however, without Yeshua it is incomplete and yet to realise its full potential.

In Romans 11 Paul asks: "Has God rejected his people?" For Jewish People and the Church, this is one of the biggest controversies that has continued to fuel the phenomena of Anti-Judaism and inadvertently contributed to Anti-Semitism and Jew-hatred.

Anti-Zionism while not directly linked to the question of whether God has rejected the Jewish people [Israel], helps any negative suggestion to contribute to an antipathy towards Jews, Judaism and Israel.

Dr. Michael Green says,

"Israel's status is claimed: The Jew would have four main grievances... In the first place, [her] status as Israel has been appropriated by the Christians. This followed naturally from their conversation about Jesus as Messiah, his followers must be true Israel... The Messiah was inconceivable apart from his flock. Jesus fulfilled the prophecies of the Old Testament, and his people were therefore heirs to all its promises. This meant, those Jews who did not put their faith in Jesus were renegades from the true Israel; they may be Jews outwardly, but were not so at heart." (Green, M, 1970:99).

Consequently many Christians lacked compassion, and they turned to having a hostile attitude not only to those Jews who rejected Jesus, but they went much further in both appropriating everything that was sacred to Judaism and then had the audacity to claim that the church had replaced Israel. In addition, they condemned them as "renegades" and not true Jews at all. The Church then claimed to be the true "Israel of God," and *old Israel* (the Jews) was rejected.

Personally speaking

I personally have met many well-meaning Christians who, when Judaism is spoken about as a religion, display a very negative attitude towards it. Part of the problem is the perception that because of Israel's failure as a whole to embrace Jesus/Yeshua as Messiah and Lord, it is supposed that God must have rejected Israel as a consequence of her failure.

It is not surprising that this negative attitude of early Christianity is still perpetuated in many circles right down to the present day. In addition, their theology concerning the Jews and the law is ill-informed and based upon a superficial understanding of the place of the law in biblical New Testament texts. Their exposure to Judaism is often based solely upon their reading of the Holy Scriptures and particularly the controversies that Yeshua and his disciples experienced with the religious leaders of the time, in the Gospels, Acts and Epistles.

Also, they usually have never met, discussed or dialogued with a Jew who practises their faith about the importance of the Torah. Prejudice fuelled by ignorance results in negative outcomes that build barriers, rather than building bridges of understanding and love.

Has God rejected Israel?

Contrary to all who have said that God has no further plan for Israel or the Jewish people, Paul, in Romans 11, deals head-on with the question, "Has God rejected his people?"

He gives a very clear unequivocal answer: "By no means! I myself am an Israelite, a descendant of Abraham, a member of the tribe of Benjamin. ² God has not rejected his people whom he foreknew" (NRSV).

The whole of Romans chapter 11 outlines Paul's thinking and argument. Rejection has its implications and consequences and, in the case of Israel's response to the messianic claims about Yeshua, he has been and continues to be a major cause of stumbling to the majority of Jewish people. However, there are growing numbers of Jews who have made the great discovery that Yeshua is more than just a prophet, a great man, miracle-working rabbi, visionary, elder brother or friend. They have concluded that he is both Messiah and Lord.

We are witnessing a greater openness and willingness on the part of Jewish people to engage in meaningful dialogue. This is not just for the sake of being nice to each other, but there is a growing thirst being expressed by many to know personally who is Yeshua of Nazareth.

> "Ask and it will be given to you; seek and you will find; knock and the door will be opened to you"
> (Matthew 7.7 – NIV).

∗

Roni Mechanic

Mahatma Gandhi

"I worship God as Truth only.
I have not yet found Him,
But I am seeking after Him." [48]

Graphic created by Roni Mechanic ©

15 — Mahatma Gandhi on an insufficient atonement

Though he was neither Jewish nor Christian, as a Hindu, Mohandas Karamchand Gandhi raised questions concerning the efficacy of the atonement that reaches to the heart of the matter. He complained that he felt that Christ's atonement was insufficient. Gandhi strove for a state of sinlessness. His contention was that, though Yeshua takes away sins and offers forgiveness, Gandhi wanted to conquer the "sin principle." This, he held, was not achieved in the atonement as proclaimed in the gospel message which was presented by those who sought to convince him.

This helps to explain some of the rigorous asceticism that Gandhi practised. He went to extreme lengths in order to force himself into submission to achieve a state of "sinless perfection." The question of the atonement (*at-one-ment*) is of the utmost importance for all devout people who seek to overcome and conquer sin and be at peace with God.

In Gandhi's book *An Autobiography, or My Experiments with Truth*, (2007) he speaks about his friendship with a Mr Coates a devout Christian, and their extended and challenging dialogue,

"He had no regard for my religion (as a Hindu). He was looking forward to delivering me from the abyss of ignorance. He wanted to convince me that, whether there was some truth in other religions, salvation was impossible for me unless I accepted Christ who represented the truth, and that my sins would not be washed away except by the intercession of Jesus, and that all good works were useless…"[49]

"Many of the contacts for which Mr Coates was responsible were good. Most struck me as being God-fearing. But during my contact with this family, one of the Plymouth Brethren confronted me with an argument for which I was not prepared":

"You cannot understand the beauty of our religion. From what you say it appears that you must be brooding over your transgressions every moment of your life, always mending them and atoning for them. How can this ceaseless cycle of action bring you redemption? You can never have peace. You admit that we are all sinners. Now look at the perfection of our belief. Our attempts at improvement and atonement are futile. And yet redemption we must have. How can we bear the burden of sin? We can but throw it on Jesus. He is the only sinless Son of God. It is his word that those who believe in him shall have everlasting life. Therein lies God's infinite mercy. And as we believe in the atonement of Jesus, our sins do not bind us. Sin we must. It is impossible to live in this world sinless. And therefore, Jesus suffered and atoned for the sins of all mankind [humankind]. Only he [she] who accepts his great redemption can have eternal peace. Think what a life of restlessness is yours, and what a promise of peace we have."

The argument utterly failed to convince me. I humbly replied:

"If this be the Christianity acknowledged by all Christians, I cannot accept it. I do not seek redemption from the consequence of my sins. I seek to be redeemed from sin itself. Until I have attained to that end, I shall be content to be restless." In addition, he says, "My difficulties lay elsewhere. They were with the Bible and its accepted inspiration."[50]

Gandhi's arguments are complex and did not simply lie with his reason for rejecting the interpretation of the message of salvation as presented by Mr Coates' Plymouth Brethren friends. The difficulties that Gandhi faced as a Hindu demonstrates that, equally, practising Jews have difficulty with the New Testament message as interpreted by all who hold to the theological stance that Christians and Messianic believers assign to Jesus as redeemer and Lord who made atonement for sin. Equally Jewish people face the accusation that their religion is trapped not in the abyss of ignorance, but none the less in bondage to the law. These kinds of accusations do not aid dialogue, but rather serve to alienate those with whom we seek to communicate what we believe.

In a similar vein, concerning the question of redemption, the use of the Hebrew Bible is essential in making sense of any New Testament discussion about the subject of the Atonement, I wish to quote from Isaiah 53.10-12 (NRSV):

[10] Yet it was the will of the LORD to crush him with pain. When you make his life an offering for sin, he shall see his offspring, and shall prolong his days; through him the will of the LORD shall prosper. [11] Out of his anguish he shall see light; he shall find satisfaction through his knowledge. The righteous one, my servant, shall make many righteous, and he shall bear their iniquities. [12] Therefore I will allot him a portion with the great, and he shall divide the spoil with the strong; because he poured out himself to death, and was

numbered with the transgressors; yet he bore the sin of many, and made intercession for the transgressors.

KJV: [10] Yet it pleased the LORD to bruise him; he hath put him to grief: when thou shalt make his soul an offering for sin, he shall see his seed, he shall prolong his days, and the pleasure of the LORD shall prosper in his hand. [11] He shall see of the travail of his soul, and shall be satisfied: by his knowledge shall my righteous servant justify many; for he shall bear their iniquities. [12] Therefore will I divide him a portion with the great, and he shall divide the spoil with the strong; because he hath poured out his soul unto death: and he was numbered with the transgressors; and he bare the sin of many, and made intercession for the transgressors.

NRSV: he shall find "satisfaction" through his knowledge.

KJV: He shall see of the travail of his soul and shall be "satisfied."

The words "satisfied" or "satisfaction" in verse 11 speak of the all-sufficiency, satisfaction or adequacy of the atoning death of the 'Suffering Servant of God.' Gandhi failed to grasp the reality that humanly speaking it is impossible to achieve "sinless perfection" in this mortal life. His struggle is not unique as many of the tzadikim (Jewish holy ones) equally struggle with a deep sense of personal need to be found righteous before a Holy God. This quotation indicates his desire to worship God, yet he strikes a note of unfulfillment:

> "I worship God as Truth only.
> I have not yet found Him,

But I am seeking after Him."[51]

Gandhi is not alone in his wistfulness, for many genuine seekers desire to know God in a deeper way, whether Jew or Gentile. Each have the same basic need to be known by God and to know him, to be loved by him and to find fulfilment and his peace.

On the question raised by Gandhi about the insufficiency of the atonement, this is equally an issue that needs be resolved in Jewish-Christian inter-faith understanding for, in addition to the question of the approach to the Law, the Atonement is a central issue. This is due to the Christian assertion that Jesus/Yeshua, as the Suffering Servant of the LORD, made atonement for sin and God was, according to Isaiah 53.12, "Satisfied!" Jewish partners in dialogue, however, accommodating that they may be, cannot easily accept this Christian affirmation and remain content, i.e. satisfied.

The significance of understanding the concepts of 'propitiation' or 'expiation,' influences the choice of words that English translations of Isaiah uses on 53:10 (KJV), "Yet it pleased the LORD to bruise him; he hath put him to grief: when thou shalt make his soul an offering for sin:

'Propitiation' describes the important aspect of Messiah's suffering, emphasizing the element of divine wrath and it differs from expiation (making amends) for sin. Yeshua bore God's wrath in our place and not only made amends for the consequence of sin. He is the 'sin' bearer.

The propitiatory or expiatory nature of Yeshua's death on the cursed tree (cross) is often poorly understood in much of contemporary theological discussion, and as a result, the notion of the sacrificial atonement of Messiah is minimised, misunderstood or excluded altogether. Gandhi was not alone in his misunderstanding of the significance of what Yeshua achieved in his atoning sacrifice.[52]

Careful attention needs to be given to the Scriptures to attain a full picture of what the death of the Messiah/Christ achieved. Both undue expectations and misunderstanding concerning the nature of the atonement has all too often characterised this subject. We need to answer the question:

Is the atoning death of Yeshua essential?

Not only do we need to answer this question, but we also need to understand that without his sacrificial death there can be no other possibility of human forgiveness and atonement. This is the witness and testimony of the whole of Holy Scripture that humankind is lost in sin and we each must face the consequences of that state that we find ourselves in - [23] "For the wages of sin is death, but the free gift of God is eternal life in Christ Jesus our Lord" (Romans 6:23 - ESV).

The writer of Hebrews says, "In fact, the law requires that nearly everything be cleansed with blood, and without the shedding of blood there is no forgiveness" (Hebrew 9:22 – NIV).

The Holy Name

ヨYヨג

ヨYヨz

יהוה

16 — "I AM" of the Tetragrammaton

Do not forget in John 8:58: Jesus said to them, "Very truly, I tell you, before Abraham was, I am." (NRSV).

This also indicates that Yeshua equates himself with the "I AM" of the Tetragrammaton – the Hebrew name of God transliterated in four letters as YHWH or JHVH and articulated as Yahweh:

יהוה

The question arises as to how to say and write the Holy Name? Out of deference for the Holy Name, observant Jews do not attempt to pronounce it and substitute *Ha Shem*, which is literally *The Name*. Because of the difficulty of knowing how to pronounce the Tetragrammaton – YHWH, most bible translators write it as LORD in English.

Jehovah is a Latinization of the Hebrew יְהֹוָה and an attempt at the vocalization of the Tetragrammaton יהוה (YHWH), the proper name of the God of Israel in the Hebrew Bible and one of the seven names of God in Judaism.

Jehovah is quite incorrect and any attempts to construct a word that approximates the YHWH should be avoided. More recent attempts have rendered it as Yahweh and an example of this is used in the Jerusalem Bible which is a Catholic translation of the Scriptures.

Holy Name groups tend to be obsessive about the use of the Tetragrammaton and are prone to a sectarianism that is divisive. I encountered such a troublesome group in Cape Town, South Africa while leading the Messianic Jewish congregation Beit Ariel. They even had their own torturous translation of the Bible called *The Scriptures*.[53]

There are also attempts at rendering the name as *Yahuweh*. However, it is best to avoid any theologically and linguistically unsound renderings of the Holy Name. The use of LORD in English language translations is a preferred way of writing or saying the Name, and L_RD in its written form will give the least offense to observant Jewish readers. The New Testament however does not use the Tetragrammaton – YHWH – for God's holy name.

The Greek New Testament text's use of Kyrios or kurios – κύριος, is usually translated as "Lord"/"lord" or "master." In religious usage, it is sometimes translated as God. It is used in the Septuagint translation of the Hebrew Bible and the Greek New Testament. Kyrios appears about 740 times in the New Testament, usually referring to Jesus.[54]

Let us be clear, the Holy Name is not to be used as a talisman, esoteric password, or magic incantation. Those who have fallen into the use of God's name in this particular way are in danger of a form of Gnosticism and, though inadvertently, they have put themselves into bondage. No one group or sect has a monopoly of the use of God's Holy Name.

Foolishness and unsound linguistic acrobatics do a disservice to the integrity of the Scriptures. Translations from the original biblical Hebrew or Aramaic into English need to be done with great care by those scholars who understand the original language and its usage. It is important to handle these sacred words with reverence and care.

Jesus' "I AM" statements in John:

4:26	Jesus said to her, "I am he, the one who is speaking to you."
6:35	Jesus said to them, "I am the bread of life. Whoever comes to me will never be hungry, and whoever believes in me will never be thirsty."
6:41	Then the Jews began to complain about him because he said, "I am the bread that came down from heaven."
6:48	I am the bread of life.
6:51	I am the living bread that came down from heaven.
8:12	Again Jesus spoke to them, saying, "I am the light of the world. Whoever follows me will never walk in darkness but will have the light of life."
8:23	He said to them, "You are from below, I am from above; you are of this world, I am not of this world."
8:24	"I told you that you would die in your sins, for you will die in your sins unless you believe that I am he."

8:28	So Jesus said, "When you have lifted up the Son of Man, then you will realise that I am he, and that I do nothing on my own, but I speak these things as the Father instructed me."
8:58	Jesus said to them, "Very truly, I tell you, before Abraham was, I am."
9:5	"As long as I am in the world, I am the light of the world."
10:9	I am the gate/door; whoever enters by me will be saved.
10:11	I am the good shepherd. The good shepherd lays down his life for the sheep.
10:30	"The Father and I are one." [form is different because the subject is plural]
10:36	"Can you say that the one whom the Father has sanctified and sent into the world is blaspheming because I said, 'I am God's Son'?"
10:38	"But if I do them, even though you do not believe me, believe the works, so that you may know and understand that the Father is in me and I am in the Father."
11:25	Jesus said to her, "I am the resurrection and the life. Those who believe in me, even though they die, will live,"

13:19	"I tell you this now, before it occurs, so that when it does occur, you may believe that I am he."
14:6	Jesus said to him, "I am the way, and the truth, and the life. No one comes to the Father except through me."
15:1	"I am the true vine, and my Father is the vine-grower."
18:5	They answered, "Jesus of Nazareth." Jesus replied, "I am he."
18:8	Jesus answered, "I told you that I am he. So, if you are looking for me, let these men go."

Yeshua is fully human, but equally he is fully divine – he is the God-man. The concept of the unity or tri-unity of God is a complex one and believers have at times been accused as tri-theists – a belief in three gods. Although the word Trinity is not declared in Scripture, the concept is implicit in the Hebrew Bible (OT) and is explicit in the New Testament. Father, Son and Holy Spirit – One God with three persons. The creed says that they are co-equal and co-eternal.

This is a difficult concept for many Jewish people to accept. Even within the Messianic movement the problem of the Ebonite heresy has resurfaced.

Ebionites in Greek: Ἐβιωναῖοι, Ebionaioi, derived from Hebrew אביונים ebyonim/ebionim, meaning 'the poor' or 'poor ones' and this is a patristic term referring to a Jewish

Christian movement that existed during the early centuries with the emergence of the various expressions of the new messianic movements of Jews who had embraced Yeshua as Messiah. They regarded Yeshua/Jesus of Nazareth as the Messiah while they rejected his divinity and his virgin birth. They insisted on the necessity of following the Jewish law and rites.[55]

While it is important to adhere to an orthodox expression of faith, there is considerable latitude as to how one may give expression to that important doctrine of the Messianic faith. The teaching in the 13 Articles of the Jewish faith as formulated by Maimonides (Rambam), the second article says, "I believe with complete faith that the Creator, blessed is His Name, is unique, and *there is no uniqueness like His in any way,* and that He alone is our G-d, Who was, Who is, and Who always will be." (https://www.interfaith.org/community/threads/2121/)

Jewish people struggle to grasp and accept the concept of the Trinity because of the rabbinic interpretation of the Shema which stresses that God is One. Also in Judaism he cannot be perceived of as having a divine Son. This is one of the reasons that Ebonism has resurfaced in its approach to the person of Yeshua HaMashiach and particularly, the question of his divinity. There is a very real danger of embracing a form of doctrine that is biblically unsound and heretical. This results in a sub-Messianic interpretation of who Yeshua is and consequently results in diminishing his place in the Godhead. From a Messianic perspective, he is more than just the Jewish Messiah, he is both Lord and God as well. To deny one of these aspects of his nature, always results in a diminishing of his role.

17 — The place of prayer

The place of prayer for both Jews and Christians shows an awareness of the human need to know that humankind is not alone in the universe, but that God is there, and he is not silent. It has been said that prayer is like breathing – with every breath that we inhale, we breath in the Spirit of God, and with every breath that we exhale it is like saying a prayer.

Acknowledging that God speaks to humankind in diverse ways, as expressed by the Jewish philosopher Franz Rosenzweig, here is a sample of such a prayer that he gives,

"Let my prayer and your love not be turned away from me – Lass mein Gebet und deine Liebe nicht von mir weichen" – that approximates to the prayer of Psalm 66.20: "Blessed is God who has not turned away my prayer, or His faithful care from me." "When you search for me, you will find me; if you seek me with all your heart…" "As a cry the prayer is a wish (wünschen) for the coming of the kingdom through actual praying (wirkliches Beten) over and beyond the power/ability of praying that is the ultimate gift of revelation unaided by redemption."[56]

An open heart accompanied by earnest prayer, will yield the fruit of righteousness and, therefore, we can learn from Franz Rosenzweig's sincere desire to know and to be known by God.

Surely, the love of the Father does hear the prayer of those who turn to him? We are told in Jeremiah 29:13 (NRSV):

"When you search for me, you will find me; if you seek me with all your heart…"

With the advent of Yeshua, the divine Son, he has become the source of divine life and speech and revelation. For just as of old God spoke through the prophets, in these last days, he speaks through his Son:

Hebrews 1 (NRSV) – God Has Spoken by His Son: [1] Long ago God spoke to our ancestors in many and various ways by the prophets, [2] but in these last days he has spoken to us by a Son, whom he appointed heir of all things, through whom he also created the worlds. [3] He is the reflection of God's glory and the exact imprint of God's very being, and he sustains all things by his powerful word. When he had made purification for sins, he sat down at the right hand of the Majesty on high, [4] having become as much superior to angels as the name he has inherited is more excellent than theirs.

This echoes the Lord's Prayer that Yeshua taught his follower to say, in Matthew 6 (NRSV),

> [9] Pray then in this way:
> Our Father in heaven,
> hallowed be your name.
> [10] Your kingdom come.
> Your will be done,
> on earth as it is in heaven.
> [11] Give us this day our daily bread.
> [12] And forgive us our debts,
> as we also have forgiven our debtors.
> [13] and do not bring us to the time of trial,
> but rescue us from the evil one.

This prayer that is universally said by Messianic believers/Christians is a very Jewish prayer and accords equally with the Jewish longing for the manifestation of the Kingdom of Heaven here on earth. A prayer for the coming of the kingdom lies at the heart of all those who desire to see the reign of God established in this age. This desire is universally shared with all people – Jews, Christians and all others of true faith. A better world where humanity will live together in peace and harmony is at the heart of all who desire the reign of God as sovereign establishing his kingdom of righteousness and justice. This reign is not only requested for by those who pray for this present time, but there is the heart's cry that his kingdom may come and that his will is done on earth as it is in heaven.

We should not minimise the importance of prayer as it is part of our human endeavour to reach out to the God who is there and longs for all to know him. Even the cry of our hearts is heard by him: "Oh, God help me!" And he will answer these pleas of desperation in the darkest hour of human need. He is there and he will come to our rescue.

Though we may struggle to articulate our thoughts in prayer, to utter the simplest of prayers, when they are said in sincerity and truth, they will prevail. In this way I have personally learnt to give expression to my deepest longings and thoughts. At times these are said with stammering lips and the deepest of sighing but, nonetheless, what is important is not the purity of speech but the sincerity of heart. An opening to God is created when we pray in this manner. Openness is that willingness to lay aside our preconceptions and prejudices as to how prayer is meant to work. I have to learn to let go and let God do his work within me. This is a principle that needs to be revisited from time to time in order not to get trapped in a rut. "New every morning is your love."

The Jesus prayer

A Russian Orthodox Psychologist, Dr Albert S Rossi, of St Vladimir's Seminary, Director of Counselling and Psychological Services says, "Prayer is not optional." Those who attended the seminar on the Jesus Prayer found it a very profound experience and a layman at the Summer Institute, wrote the 'Jesus Prayer' itself was the most important thing he learned all week. In its classical form the Jesus Prayer is, "Lord Jesus Christ, Son of God, have mercy on me, a sinner." The actual words of our short prayers can vary. We might say the classic version of the Jesus Prayer, or we might say, "Lord Jesus Christ, have mercy on me."

We may say, "Lord Jesus, have mercy" or, we might say a Psalm verse, or a Bible quote, or some other prayer. Monks of old said, "Lord, make haste to help me. Lord, make speed to save me," all day long. The history of the Jesus Prayer dates back to the early sixth century. Diadochos, a fifth-century ascetic whose works are included in the Philokalia, taught that repetition of the prayer leads to inner stillness. Even earlier John Cassian recommended this type of prayer and also, in Egypt, Nitria, short "arrow" prayers, were practiced. Abba Macarius said that with few words it is enough to hold out your hands and say, "Lord, according to your desire and your wisdom, have mercy." If pressed in the struggle, say, "Lord, save me!" or say, "Lord." He knows what is best for us and will have mercy upon us.[57]

My Messianic Jewish adaptation:

The longest form:
"Yeshua the Messiah,
Son of God have mercy upon me!"

This may be reduced to:
"Yeshua, have mercy upon me!"

And a further reduction:
"Yeshua!"

I have found this type of meditative prayer very uplifting and helpful in giving me a sense of harmony and connectedness with God, helping to still me in the midst of a very busy day. Mindfulness helps one to find quiet and solitude in everyday life.

"Lord Jesus Christ, Son of God, have mercy on me, a sinner": In this extended form of the Jesus Prayer there are some important elements about the making of a profession of faith in Yeshua and as Messiah and Lord. No one can sincerely say this prayer without an acknowledgement that one believes that Yeshua is both the Messiah of Israel and the divine Son of God. It becomes more obvious what this entails as you read my Personal Account in the next chapter.

Liturgical prayer

In both Judaism and the Christian/Messianic faith, liturgical prayer plays a big part in both the private devotional life of the believer as well as in public worship. From a Jewish perspective, Jewish Prayer books contain a wealth of prayers that cover every aspect of life. As in the cycle of life, the Jewish adherent is taught and encouraged to offer prayers from the time of rising in the morning to the end of the day when before one goes to sleep. From a Christian viewpoint, depending on the particular denomination and tradition, both formal liturgical prayers, as well as free spontaneous and extemporaneous prayers are also encouraged.

The Roman Catholic, Anglican, Lutheran; Orthodox and Coptic Churches each have their prescribed prayer books and, as in Judaism, so they too have fashioned prayers to cover the whole spectrum of life. The Hebrew Scriptures and particularly the Psalms play a significant role in both Jewish and Christian worship. The Jewish writings of their sages and rabbis give rich sources of prayers and these have found their way into Jewish public worship and private devotion. Christians have made use of material from Jewish sources as well as from material from the OT deuterocanonical books. These include Tobit; Judith; Wisdom; Tobit; Sirach; Baruch; 1 & 2 Maccabees; Jubilees, Ecclesiasticus.[58]

The New Testament Scriptures are also a rich resource of prayers that have been incorporated into both psalmody and liturgical prayers. Prayer is not only spiritually but also psychologically beneficial to those who pray regularly. This is attested to by psychologists, therapists, rabbis, priests and pastors alike. It contributes to a greater sense of well-being and wholeness. It contributes to one's self-care and an inner sense of inner calm and contentment. We should not only view prayer as something that we do when we are in need or facing a crisis, but giving expression to gratitude and thankfulness should also be a part of one's daily prayers.

18 — My personal account

Arguments are raised against attempting to lead Jewish people to faith in Yeshua. These are not new or unique; they have been used numerous times by Jewish family and community members by equating Hitler, the Pope and Billy Graham in their efforts to destroy the Jewish people.

A Jewish friend who had made a profession of faith but had turned back from following Yeshua as Messiah and Lord, said to me: "Come back to your own people* and leave these Christians!" דיין און מענטשן – Yiddish: "dien eigenen menchen/ German: Ihre eigenen Leute."

He arranged for me to meet a young rabbi from Gibraltar who was working at the Kol El Orthodox Jewish Centre in Observatory, Johannesburg. The rabbi, then said to me:

"We have lost six million Jewish people to the Nazis, and now with your embracing Jesus, it is six million and one!" He also said that it was in ignorance that I had come to my decision to follow this false Gentile god and that I had been deceived into following this "Yeshu." Yeshu is an acronym for: "May His name be blotted out!" and is used to dissuade Jewish people from belief in him.

The rabbi then quoted Deuteronomy 18[20] "But any prophet who speaks in the name of other gods, or who presumes to speak in my name a word that I have not commanded the prophet to speak – that prophet shall die.'[21] You may say to yourself, 'How can we recognise a word that the Lord has not spoken?' [22] If a prophet speaks in the name of the Lord but the thing does not take place or prove true, it is a word that the Lord has not spoken. The prophet has spoken it presumptuously; do not be frightened by it." (NRSV)

He told me to read this passage aloud, and then he said to me, "this is your Jesus, for God is testing you." It was a true body blow to my recent commitment to follow Yeshua, not having a full intellectual understanding of my new-found faith. However, I was not able to deny that I had experienced a profound sense of God's presence when I had made my profession of faith a short while before. Later that evening while attending a worship service a young woman stood to sing a song to the congregation, and when she enunciated the words, "that lovely name of Jesus," though my mind was in a turmoil, in the depth of my inner being, "I knew that I knew." This was beyond reasoning, but not unreasonable.

There is a chorus line used in a worship song that goes like this: "I have decided to follow Jesus, no turning back, no turning back."

This is my testimony to the spiritual reality that I had experienced as a Jew who had found faith in the God of Abraham, Isaac and Jacob, and the God and Father of Yeshua the Messiah.

The same God for the Jews and Christians

If, as Will Herberg a well-respected American Jewish theologian said, he is the same God for the Jewish people as well as for the Christians, then the contention by that young rabbi from Gibraltar who said that I had been led astray was wrong. On further reflection upon the passage from

Deuteronomy 18: [20] But any prophet who speaks in the name of other gods," If the rabbi had quoted the text fully, then it is in fact a prophetic reference to "A New Prophet Like Moses."

Deuteronomy 18: [14] The nations you will dispossess listen to those who practice sorcery or divination. But as for you, the LORD your God has not permitted you to do so. [15] The LORD your God will raise up for you a prophet like me from among you, from your fellow Israelites. You must listen to him. [16] For this is what you asked of the LORD your God at Horeb on the day of the assembly when you said, "Let us not hear the voice of the LORD our God nor see this great fire anymore, or we will die."

[17] The LORD said to me: "What they say is good. [18] I will raise up for them a prophet like you from among their fellow Israelites, and I will put my words in his mouth. He will tell them everything I command him. [19] I myself will call to account anyone who does not listen to my words that the prophet speaks in my name. [20] But a prophet who presumes to speak in my name anything I have not commanded, or a prophet who speaks in the name of other gods, is to be put to death." (NIV)

The rabbi's contention was that I had been led away from the God of Israel to some foreign god of the Gentiles. However, was this not my experience of my encounter with Yeshua of whom Moses spoke? Yeshua is declared to be a Prophet like Moses, whom God would send to his people Israel.

What does the Scripture say in regard to sharing the Gospel with Jewish people?

In its original proclamation the Good News was to the Jewish people and it was proclaimed by a Jew to their own kith and kin. Yeshua said that he had come to the lost sheep of the house of Israel.

We read in Matthew 15: [21] Then Jesus went thence, and departed into the coasts of Tyre and Sidon. [22] And, behold, a woman of Canaan came out of the same coasts, and cried unto him, saying, "Have mercy on me, O Lord, thou Son of David; my daughter is grievously vexed with a devil." [23] But he answered her not a word. And his disciples came and besought him, saying, "Send her away; for she crieth after us." [24] But he answered and said, "I am not sent but unto the lost sheep of the house of Israel." [25] Then came she and worshipped him, saying, "Lord, help me." [26] But he answered and said, "It is not meet to take the children's bread, and to cast it to dogs." [27] And she said, "Truth, Lord: yet the dogs eat of the crumbs which fall from their masters' table." [28] Then Jesus answered and said unto her, "O woman, great is thy faith: be it unto thee even as thou wilt." And her daughter was made whole from that very hour. (KJV)

It would appear that Yeshua not only said that his message was exclusively for Jews, but he even insulted the woman by saying that it was not right to give the children's food to the dogs. However, this Gentile woman in her desperation was willing to put up with being rebuffed by Yeshua, in order that her daughter might get healed from this Jewish miracle working healer and rabbi. Consequently, Yeshua granted her request by healing her daughter and he commended her for her faith.

The Apostle Paul in his letter to the Romans 1:[16] "For I am not ashamed of the gospel of Christ: for it is the power of God unto salvation to everyone that believeth; to the Jew first, and also to the Greek. [17] For therein is the righteousness of God revealed from faith to faith: as it is written, 'The just shall live by faith.'" (KJV)

In John 10:16 we read, "And other sheep I have, which are not of this fold: them also I must bring, and they shall hear my voice; and there shall be one-fold, and one shepherd." (KJV)

Though not explicitly expressed, Yeshua implied that his focus was broadening beyond the narrow focus of just the Jewish people. Yeshua's focus upon the Jewish people was now clearly broadened when he commissioned his disciples just prior to his ascension, "But ye shall receive power, after that the Holy Ghost is come upon you: and ye shall be witnesses unto me both in Jerusalem, and in all Judaea, and in Samaria, and unto the uttermost part of the earth." (Acts 1.8 KJV): Jerusalem and Judea – Jews; Samaria – half-Jews; and the ends of the earth – Gentiles. With this progression he showed that his outlook and the scope of their proclamation had extended beyond its narrow focus upon Israel.

So, should I share the Good News?

My close family said, "it is enough that you believe in this Jesus, but please keep it within the confines of the family!" To some degree, I did not say anything to my wider family and members of the local Jewish community, but I did not totally comply by keeping it completely to myself. For I read the words of Yeshua, when he said, that if you deny me before others, I will deny you before my Father in heaven. I faced a dilemma as to whether I was to fully comply with my parent's wishes and disobey Yeshua's command to be a witness? It is difficult to keep a secret, particularly if it is not something to be ashamed of or wanting to hide from others.

Hillbrow, Johannesburg, was like Soho, London and Canal Street, Manchester, UK or Greenwich Village, NY, USA, with its late-night bars, cinemas, restaurants and night clubs. There was a covered shopping precinct, called Highpoint Shopping Centre, with an upstairs cinema complex and a downstairs 24-hour deli. It was a very popular location. When the cinema show was over, folk would come down to the deli to purchase food to take home.

I was part of an informal group of young people who could best be described as "street preachers."

We gathered near the entrance to the centre particularly on a Friday night and a Saturday and gave impromptu sermons that lasted between five and ten minutes. We had watched Billy Graham gospel films that showed him preaching with an open leather-bound King James Bible, and he would hold this aloft in one hand and loudly proclaim in a booming voice, "the Bible says…" The pages of the bible would gently flap in the breeze as he spoke. He became our role-model and we copied his style of proclamation. When it was my turn to preach, I stood there with an open bible in one hand and began to deliver my short message at the moment that the cinema show had just ended. Down the side steps of the centre came my dad's friend Harry, a Jewish man who also worked in the garment trade together with my dad. He saw me standing there in full flight. Though he did not come over to where we were standing, he hovered on the steps for a few moments taking in this apparition of me preaching.

On Sunday morning the phone rang in the Mechanic's household and I heard my dad saying on the phone, "Yes, Harry that was Roni that you saw last night." Followed by more muted comments about not wanting to say anything more about his Jewish evangelist preaching son.

Slowly, but surely the word was getting out about Roni Mechanic the Jewish preacher. Then the bomb dropped for all of the Jewish community in South Africa to read. My story was told in a report in "The Sunday Express."[59]

There was no more need for me to keep a low profile and nowhere to hide, not that I wanted to hide anymore. I, together with the Apostle Paul, have to say, "I am not ashamed of the gospel, for it is the power of God unto salvation, to the Jew first and also the Greek." (Romans 1.16 KJV)

It was never my intention to cause pain or discomfort to my Jewish family, friends or the wider Jewish community. However, I could not live as a secret believer, never breathing a word to anyone, for that would be a betrayal of the very tenets of the gospel message. For if it is good news to be shared, then it is good news for everyone – Jew and Gentile alike. If in honouring God others do not like what I have said, then it is not I who am to blame. However, I feel a sense of godly sorrow for those who have closed their hearts to this message of hope as contained in the gospel of salvation as proclaimed by Yeshua and others.

Paul says in Romans 9: [1] "I say the truth in Christ, I lie not, my conscience also bearing me witness in the Holy Ghost, [2] That I have great heaviness and continual sorrow in my heart. [3] For I could wish that myself were accursed from Christ for my brethren, my kinsmen according to the flesh." (KJV)

19 — The power of the Gospel

PAUL - ROMANS 1:16-17 (NKJV), [16] "For I am not ashamed of the gospel of Christ, for it is the power of God to salvation for everyone who believes, for the Jew first and also for the Greek. [17] For in it the righteousness of God is revealed from faith to faith; as it is written, "The just shall live by faith.""

In Jewish religious circles there is almost a universal rejection of any attempt to proclaim the Gospel to Jewish people. This is seen as proselytising and it is strongly condemned and actively opposed.

An eminent inter-faith advocate, Rabbi Yechiel Eckstein took this position and rejected any form of Jewish evangelism. He opposed Messianic Jews and Christians that uphold the belief in the necessity of its proclamation. This rabbi is not alone in this stance and opposition to Jewish evangelism. A necessary response to Yechiel Eckstein, Franz Rosenzweig, Will Herberg, and company is appropriate.

Dr Louis Goldberg a Messianic Jewish scholar from the USA in his essay, *"Are there Two Ways of Atonement? Confronting the Controversies,* (1992), gives a critique of Dr Franz Rosenzweig the Jewish philosopher, that equally applies to Dr Will Herberg. Dr Goldberg says,

"Such being the case, we can understand why Rabbi Eckstein can use the two-covenant theory as his basic argument to demonstrate that any mission to convert Jewish people is at best, unnecessary (Jewish people and Christians should respect each other's expression of faith), and, at worst, a nasty business (it gravely harms the identity and existence of Jewish people by decimating their ranks). This point is especially powerful when considering the six million who perished in the Holocaust." [60]

Hence the use of very emotive language like, committing "spiritual genocide," "snatching Jewish souls," and, as the Gibraltar rabbi said to me, "We have lost six million Jewish people to the Nazis, and now with your embracing Jesus, it is six million and one!" It will always have its desired effect of engendering anger and revolution on the part of Jewish people and guilt and shame on the part of Christians. The consequence of this type of frontal attack will militate against any possibility of true dialogue and will serve only to reinforce entrenched positions of mutual hostility and mistrust.

In Franz Rosenzweig's and Will Herberg's arguments for the dual-covenant approach, it was certainly not their intention to accuse those Christians engaged in sharing their faith with Jewish people of being dishonest. This is in sharp contrast to Rabbi Eckstein who painted his canvas in broad brush strokes. Equally, the Kol El rabbi from Gibraltar that I encountered, gave attention to the specific detail of contending with my decision to follow Yeshua as Messiah and Lord. These rabbis do not harbour malicious intent but are motivated by a genuine concern for "the lost Jewish soul."

However, Will Herberg is very strong on the issue of the importance of our theology being "biblically" rooted – the Hebrew Scriptures for Jew and both the "Old and New Testaments" for Christians. Particularly the New Testament has a lot to say about the importance of mission and evangelism. This needs further comment. With this in mind as we turn to the New Testament we are presented with what the Scripture actually says.

A major theme of Paul's Epistle to the Romans, so far as salvation is concerned, is that God views Jews and Gentiles as equal before him:

Romans 2:7-12: [7] to those who by patiently doing good seek for glory and honour and immortality, he will give eternal life; [8] while for those who are self-seeking and who obey not the truth but wickedness, there will be wrath and fury. [9] There will be anguish and distress for everyone who does evil, the Jew first and also the Greek, [10] but glory and honour and peace for everyone who does good, the Jew first and also the Greek. [11] For God shows no partiality. (NRSV)

Galatians 5:3 has been used by those who support dual-covenant theology. However, there is a problem with this as it actually says, "You have been severed from Christ, you who seek to be justified by law; you have fallen from grace." (5:15) And this should be considered together with Galatians 2:21 "I do not nullify the grace of God, for if righteousness comes through the Law, then Christ died needlessly."

Similarly, when Paul had to rebuke the Apostle Peter at Antioch: Galatians 2:[11] But when Cephas came to Antioch, I opposed him to his face, because he stood self-condemned; [12] for until certain people came from James, he used to eat with the Gentiles. But after they came, he drew back and kept himself separate for fear of the circumcision faction. [13] And the other Jews joined him in this hypocrisy, so that even Barnabas was led astray by their hypocrisy. [14] But when I saw that they were not acting consistently with the truth of the gospel, I said to Cephas before them all, "If you, though a Jew, live like a Gentile and not like a Jew, how can you compel the Gentiles to live like Jews?" (NRSV)

Jews and Gentiles are saved by faith

Galatians 2:[15] We ourselves are Jews by birth and not Gentile sinners; [16] yet we know that a person is justified not by the works of the law but through faith in Jesus Christ. And we have come to believe in Christ Jesus, so that we might be justified by faith in Christ, and not by doing the works of the law, because no one will be justified by the works of the law. [17] But if, in our effort to be justified in Christ, we ourselves have been found to be sinners, is Christ then a servant of sin? Certainly not! [18] But if I build up again the very things that I once tore down, then I demonstrate that I am a transgressor. [19] For through the law I died to the law, so that I might live to God. I have been crucified with Christ; [20] and it is no longer I who live, but it is Christ who lives in me. And the life I now live in the flesh I live by faith in the Son of God, who loved me and gave himself for me. [21] I do not nullify the grace of God; for if justification comes through the law, then Christ died for nothing. (NRSV)

Not two ways of salvation

According to sound biblical theological understanding, there is only one way of salvation that is applicable to both Jews and Gentiles alike. To teach otherwise is to deny the necessity to proclaim the good news to Jewish people and in fact it nullifies of the teaching of the New Testament.

20 — My story

My own personal story gives testimony to the strong reactions that I received from family, friends and the Jewish community at large in Johannesburg, South Africa. Anger, with shame and rejection, were just some of the issues that confronted me. My story hit the national press and was featured in the popular tabloid "The Sunday Express"[61]:

"The Christian Jews — 'We can share both faiths,' they claim." "… Mr. Mechanic, 25, a graphic artist, told me: "I have always been a searcher after truth. I grew up in a fundamentally Jewish home, but after my Bar-mitzvah my religious activities began to diminish."

"There was something missing in my religion. I read the philosophies of other people, only to become aware of more questions and no answers." "I longed for the meeting ground of all men [women], yet somehow I did not see it around me. My cry was 'if there is a God, where are you?' I matriculated [and two years later] at Art College, and [I] became appalled by the permissiveness and the depravity of the world."

"During a lecture on the designer as a communicator, a lecturer asked us what we were trying to communicate? As a Jew, he went on to say he had concluded Jesus was the Messiah of the Jewish people. My interest was aroused, and we embarked on a study of the Old Testament (Hebrew Scriptures)."

"I was amazed at the writers and prophets who foretold the coming of the Messiah. They wrote firstly about his suffering and how he would be cut off (killed) but not for himself (Daniel 9.26)."

"Mr. Mechanic's faith in Christ (Messiah) stems from a close study of the Old and New Testaments."

"It is nearly five years since I first walked the road," he said. "I have found that through my new relationship with [God], through Jesus, who makes all men[/women]… one through Jesus." …

"Young People" - Most of the Christian Jews in Johannesburg are said to number about a 100 — many of them as young people have encountered strong opposition from their parents and from rabbis…"

"But Rabbi Shapiro told me (the reporter for the Express) they represented a fringe group and were still a very small minority. They must realise too, they could not be Christians as well as being Jews – 'You can't be a member of two faiths,' he said."

Their parents were not to blame and often they did not have a good grounding in their Jewish faith and if they do, this commitment to Christ will not last, the rabbi contended.

While what Rabbi Shapiro said was a fact for some, for others they found an enduring faith, as in my case in my decision to follow Yeshua HaMashiach (Jesus the Messiah).

My profession of faith in Yeshua

Isaiah 52:13-53:12 (CJB),
52:13 "See how my servant will succeed!
He will be raised up, exalted, highly honoured!
14 Just as many were appalled at him,
because he was so disfigured
that he didn't even seem human
and simply no longer looked like a man,
15 so now he will startle many nations;
because of him, kings will be speechless.
For they will see what they had not been told,
they will ponder things they had never heard."
53:1 Who believes our report?
To whom is the arm of Adonai revealed?
2 For before him he grew up like a young plant,
like a root out of dry ground.
He was not well-formed or especially handsome;
we saw him, but his appearance did not attract us.
3 People despised and avoided him,
a man of pains, well acquainted with illness.
Like someone from whom people turn their faces,
he was despised; we did not value him.
4 In fact, it was our diseases he bore,
our pains from which he suffered;
yet we regarded him as punished,
stricken and afflicted by God.
5 But he was wounded because of our crimes,
crushed because of our sins;
the disciplining that makes us whole fell on him,
and by his bruises* (stripes/lashes) we are healed.
6 We all, like sheep, went astray;
we turned, each one, to his own way;

Roni Mechanic

yet Adonai laid on him
the guilt of all of us.
[7] Though mistreated, he was submissive —
he did not open his mouth.
Like a lamb led to be slaughtered,
like a sheep silent before its shearers,
he did not open his mouth.
[8] After forcible arrest and sentencing,
he was taken away;
and none of his generation protested
his being cut off from the land of the living
for the crimes of my people,
who deserved the punishment themselves.
[9] He was given a grave among the wicked;
in his death he was with a rich man.
Although he had done no violence
and had said nothing deceptive,
[10] yet it pleased Adonai to crush him with illness,
to see if he would present himself as a guilt offering.
If he does, he will see his offspring;
and he will prolong his days;
and at his hand Adonai's desire
will be accomplished.
[11] After this ordeal, he will see satisfaction.
"By his knowing [pain and sacrifice],
my righteous servant makes many righteous;
it is for their sins that he suffers.
[12] Therefore I will assign him a share with the great,
he will divide the spoil with the mighty,
for having exposed himself to death
and being counted among the sinners,
while actually bearing the sin of many
and interceding for the offenders."

Though the rabbis have offered various interpretations of this passage from Isaiah, none have proved that satisfactory. It was once said to me that this is a description of Jewish suffering, and while there are certainly some similarities that describe Israel's long experience of being despised and rejected by others, there does not appear to be any theological justification to say that Isaiah's Suffering Servant is the nation of Israel. The prophet clearly speaks of an individual's vicarious, self-offering of himself as a sacrificial substitute in place of the lost sheep.

Reading through the passage verse by verse, it shows how this servant of the Lord is offered up in place of the sinner and through his sacrifice he bore their iniquities and carried their sorrow and the lashes and stripes that he bore were for the healing of many, and not himself.

However badly Israel has suffered and continues to suffer, no Jewish person would reasonably want to claim that the persecution and anti-Semitism that is directed at them has any efficacious effect or merit.

While Jewish people are scapegoated and victimised, this is neither sanctioned by a loving God, nor would he want Israel to suffer on behalf of another people's wickedness.

Another and more satisfactory explanation needs be offered to convince anyone that the Jewish people are chosen by God to be the "whipping-boy" of the nations. God neither conceived that nor sanctions it. The person spoken of as the one "who made himself an offering for sin," is none other than Yeshua HaMashiah, God's only Son, whom the Father gave in the place of lost humankind. Jew and Gentile alike can find forgiveness, atonement and redemption through Yeshua's self-offering of himself in our place. He is our kaporah – atoning covering for sin and, as we turn to him, we find not only forgiveness, but healing, life and peace.

It is time to give up our feeble excuses and accept God's gracious, free unmerited gift of salvation.

My dilemma as a young Jewish person growing up in Johannesburg, was not a question of prejudice, but ignorance about the person of Yeshua. Though I knew that he came from a Jewish background, yet I knew little if anything about who he really is, what he came to do and why we as Jews did not believe in him. Slowly, but surely the mist began to clear, and the veil of blindness was being lifted from my Jewish heart in my discovery of who Israel's anointed is. It was by grace and through grace that this divine revelation was happening.

The inter-dependence of the two faiths -
What applies to the one, must surely apply to the other?

21 — The 29th May 1969

I was invited to dinner, together with a friend, by one of my lecturers, Peter Eliastam, a Messianic Jew who taught at the Johannesburg School of Art. After we ate we retired to the living room and continued our discussion concerning the Messianic claims made about Yeshua of Nazareth. Two specific passages of Scripture became our topic of discussion – Psalm 22 and Isaiah 52–53.

Peter spoke about the suffering of the Messiah as a vicarious offering for sin. The concept of the need for sins to be atoned for and human guilt to be forgiven are well known concepts in Judaism – the Jewish Day of Atonement is set aside to particularly address our failures and short comings. With fasting and prayer for an approximately twenty-five-hour period during the High and Holy days, this special day is dedicated by Jewish people throughout the world to implore God to forgive sin.

Isaiah begs the question as to who will take away our sins? He presents humankind with the Suffering Servant who was indeed wounded for our transgressions and bruised for our iniquities and the stroke that was due to us fell upon him. It is by his stripes that we are healed when he made atonement for our sins and shortcomings.

Psalm 22 tells of the desolation of the Servant of the Lord and the cry he uttered was originally said in Aramaic:

"Eli, Eli, lama sabachthani?" – "My God, My God, why have You forsaken Me?"

אלהי אלהי למא שבקתני

In addition, the psalmist says of those who tormented him:

Psalm 22 Complete Jewish Bible (CJB),
2 (1) My God! My God! Why have you abandoned me? Why so far from helping me, so far from my anguished cries? 3 (2) My God, by day I call to you, but you don't answer; likewise at night, but I get no relief. 4 (3) Nevertheless, you are holy, enthroned on the praises of Isra'el. 5 (4) In you our ancestors put their trust; they trusted, and you rescued them. 6 (5) They cried to you and escaped; they trusted in you and were not disappointed. 7 (6) But I am a worm, not a man, scorned by everyone, despised by the people. 8 (7) All who see me jeer at me; they sneer and shake their heads: 9 (8) "He committed himself to Adonai, so let him rescue him! Let him set him free if he takes such delight in him!" 10 (9) But you are the one who took me from the womb, you made me trust when I was on my mother's breasts. 11 (10) Since my birth I've been thrown on you; you are my God from my mother's womb. 12 (11) Don't stay far from me, for trouble is near; and there is no one to help. 13 (12) Many bulls surround me, wild bulls of Bashan close in on me. 14 (13) They open their mouths wide against me, like ravening, roaring lions. 15 (14) I am poured out like water; all my bones are out of joint; my heart has become like wax – it melts inside me; 16 (15) my mouth is as dry as a fragment of a pot, my tongue sticks to my palate; you lay me down in the dust of death. 17 (16) Dogs are all around me, a pack of villains closes in on me like a lion [at] my hands and feet.* 18 (17) I can count every one of my bones, while they gaze at me and gloat. 19 (18) They divide my garments among themselves; for my clothing they throw dice.

*(They pierced my hands and my feet – KJV). This is a metaphor for a lion's attack, as it would surely pierce a victim's hands and feet with its teeth.

There cannot be a more graphic description of crucifixion than given in this Psalm a thousand years before the birth of Yeshua.

A strong sense of conviction

Peter explained that God did this for me and that I personally could appropriate what the Suffering Servant had done for me. A strong sense of conviction took hold of me and I asked what I needed to do to receive God's gracious offer of deliverance? We then turned to Paul's Letter to the Roman's chapter 10:9-13: (KJV),

[9] "That if thou shalt confess with thy mouth the Lord Jesus, and shalt believe in thine heart that God hath raised him from the dead, thou shalt be saved. [10] For with the heart man believeth unto righteousness; and with the mouth confession is made unto salvation. [11] For the scripture saith, Whosoever believeth on him shall not be ashamed. [12] For there is no difference between the Jew and the Greek: for the same Lord over all is rich unto all that call upon him. [13] For whosoever shall call upon the name of the Lord shall be saved."

I responded after the reading of this passage of Scripture and said that I wanted to yield my life to God and put my trust in the Jewish Messiah, Yeshua. I prayed a prayer of commitment:

"Yeshua, if you are the Messiah of Israel and Saviour of humankind, then please come into my life and deliver me and become my Lord and mediator. Amen."

The light turned on

I was flooded with an overwhelming sense of joy and peace and I instinctively knew that my sins were forgiven, and the burden of guilt and shame were covered by the atoning sacrifice of the Messiah's sacrificial death.

Everything that the prophet Isaiah spoke about in chapter 52:13-53:12 became a reality and this was the beginning of a new life in the Messiah's kingdom.

Peter responded with the acclamation, "It is a miracle, a true miracle!"

Yeshua is God's means of redemption:

John 3:16 Complete Jewish Bible (CJB)
[16] "For God so loved the world that he gave his only and unique Son, so that everyone who trusts in him may have eternal life, instead of being utterly destroyed.

My journey to a new life in Messiah Yeshua had begun. Many questions flooded into my mind as to what were the implications that I faced. I was sailing into unchartered waters. How was my decision going to affect my identity as a Jew? What was the reaction of my family and friends going to be? These were just a few of the things that I contemplated.

New song: Amazing Grace

There is a song that goes like this, "Things are different now, something happened to me when I gave my life to him, …" A new outlook and a new song are an apt way to describe the spiritual awakening or rebirth. The Scripture describes it as being "born of God's Spirit" or "born anew." From this the expression "born again" became the catch phrase of the evangelical revival that swept the Western world during the sixties and seventies. (see John 3:16)

Theologically, the Scriptures declare that when someone turns to God and embraces the gospel, a spiritual rebirth takes place. Not only does one experience a new and deeper desire to know God, but also the desire to share that with others is also a consequence of the spiritual regeneration that is taking place.

You Must Be Born Again

John 3 (ESV),
Now there was a man of the Pharisees named Nicodemus, a ruler of the Jews. ²This man came to Jesus by night and said to him, "Rabbi, we know that you are a teacher come from God, for no one can do these signs that you do unless God is with him." ³Jesus answered him, "Truly, truly, I say to you, unless one is born again he cannot see the kingdom of God." ⁴Nicodemus said to him, "How can a man be born when he is old? Can he enter a second time into his mother's womb and be born?" ⁵Jesus answered, "Truly, truly, I say to you, unless one is born of water and the Spirit, he cannot enter the kingdom of God. ⁶That which is born of the flesh is flesh, and that which is born of the Spirit is spirit. ⁷Do not marvel that I said to you, 'You must be born again.' ⁸The wind blows where it wishes, and you hear its sound, but you do not know where it comes from or where it goes. So it is with everyone who is born of the Spirit."

Roni Mechanic

YOU MUST BE BORN AGAIN
YOU MUST BE BORN AGAIN

*

"In borrowing elements from both the Christian and Jewish worlds while refusing to acknowledge the boundary that exists between Christianity and Judaism. Messianic Jews muddy the waters…"

(Shoshana Feher)

22 — Don't muddy the waters

"Muddy Waters is best cleared by leaving it alone" [62] (Allan W. Watts).

In his recently published book, *A Profile of Jewish Believers in the UK Church* (2018), Jonathan Allen discusses Shoshana Feher's comments about how the Messianic movement is grappling with its self-identity in her book *Passing Over Easter*. "Feher talks of 'consistent inconsistency' as the movement constantly negotiates its position. Elements come from both the Christian and Jewish worlds while refusing to acknowledge the boundary that exists between Christianity and Judaism. Messianic Jews muddy the waters and cause offence to both 'parent' religions who, typically, are uncomfortable with or refuse to recognise their child. [Messianic Jews] MJS threaten the existing classification in a way that Jews who convert to Christianity don't, because the former (MJS) straddle a previously strong boundary, insisting on retaining and exercising both identities."[63]

Yet surely Messianic Jews should be allowed to self-identify? If that is a given, then are they not equally entitled to borrow elements from both the Christian and Jewish worlds? Modernity may attempt to prescribe closed systems, while post-modernity does not have such constraints built into its way of looking at the world. Pic 'n mix is the new order of the day is it not?

At my cousin's wedding soon after the Sunday Express article had been published, I met my former rabbi. When I went over to greet him out of respect, he refused to take my hand and said, "I am no longer your rabbi!" For him belief in Yeshua was an anathema for a Jew. To him I had crossed over to the other side and he was not alone in his contention that I had converted. According to the well-established view, one was either Jewish or Christian, with no possibility of there being a Messianic Jew: "The Christian Jews - 'We can share both faiths,' they claim," (Sunday Express, 1974:13) Though my former rabbi's comment hurt, on further reflection an inner voice seemed to say, "he is correct and has told you the truth, because 'Yeshua' is your rabbi (teacher) now."

More recently, while completing my M.A. studies at Manchester University, UK (2000), one of my tutors invited me to attend the annual Holocaust day seminar held at Menorah Synagogue Cheshire Reform Congregation, Sale, Manchester, UK. Gordon Thomas introduced me to Rabbi Brian Fox, saying, "I would like you to meet Mr. Mechanic who is a Messianic Jew." Rabbi Fox looked at me intently and said, "There is no such thing as a Messianic Jews You are either a Christian or a Jew. You can't be both!"

Subsequently, a few years later after I graduated, I was invited to teach Contemporary Judaism to third year undergraduate B.A. students at the Nazarene Theological College, Manchester University. I asked Rabbi Fox to co-teach part of the twelve-week course with me. He was happy to join me in instructing the students, having established that I was a "Christian" and as long as I did not refer to myself as a "Messianic Jew." Had I insisted on calling myself a "Messianic Jew" he would have refused to participate in the teaching programme. I faced a choice of either complying with his classification of "who is a Jew," or face the fact that the course would have been less effective without his valuable contribution. I compromised, complying with his classification for the benefit of the input that he made.

Shoshana Fereh has given an insightful analysis of the dilemma that confronts Messianic Jews who seek to be part of two people. Personally, it is never an easy place to be; yet I can live with this ambiguity however challenging and uncomfortable it might be.

"Push Me Pull You" (PMPY)

Defining oneself as a Messianic Jew often feels like the "Push Me Pull You" (PMPY) sports game (that requires two teams of two players each): Joined at the waist, you and your partner share a single worm-like body as you wrestle your opponent for control of the ball. It's a bit like a big hug or playing soccer with your small intestines. With every action affecting both you and your partner (and mandatory shouting) PMPY combines the best parts of co-op multiplayer with the worst parts of your last breakup.[64]

The pushmi-pullyu, pronounced "push-me—pull-you," is a "gazelle/unicorn cross" with a head at opposite ends of its body and appears in *Doctor Dolittle's Circus* and *Doctor Dolittle's Caravan*. The pushmi-pullyu usually only uses one of its heads to talk, reserving the other for eating (thus allowing it to eat while speaking without being rude) and claims that its great-grandfather was the last unicorn.

Unlike Doctor Dolittle's story of the PMPY and the last unicorn, Messianic Jews are neither mythological creatures nor relics of history. In the contemporary world, Messianic Judaism as a movement is experiencing considerable growth and its voice is increasingly being heard by a watching world and it is speaking for itself.

My fellow Jews are definitely on the "Push Me" end of the game saying, "You are no longer a Jew," while the Christian church is on the "Pull Me" away from my Jewish heritage side, preferring that I completely assimilate into the predominantly Western European Gentile culture that defines their identity. At best I am seen as an anomaly, and at worst as an oddity. I recall a Christian lady asking me whether I was Jewish or a Christian after I had given a talk at her congregation. This question was due to the fact that I wore a kippa and spoke about the Hebraic meaning behind the Passover and how Easter relates to that Jewish festival.

Inter-faith understanding

With the greatest respect for Jewish scholars, from the perspective of New Testament biblical theology, one must conclude that their dual-covenant theological positions and those of Christian theologians that concur with them, including Reinhold Niebuhr, Bishop Richard Harris (CCJ) and James Parkes, do not square up with sound New Testament hermeneutical principles. This is not to diminish the profound contribution that they have made to the field of Jewish-Christian religious relations.

But at what cost does inter-faith understanding and rapprochement come for both the Jewish and Christian faith communities? Surely it is not justified to seek a "dialogue" at any price? Rabbi Leo Baeck emphasised how important the creating of a healthy climate of greater openness is, so as to aid honest conversations between equals. A unique contribution that Buber made was his ability to communicate with others who held a different perspective on a level playing field and giving the other person the opportunity to express their point of view as an equal. With these thoughts in mind, what is true for Jewish people must be equally true for Christians. It is important for dialogue partners that no one should demand or expect the other to abandon that which is sacred to them to make dialogue work.

Therefore, when considering the integrity of the Gospel message as contained in the New Testament, to deny Jewish people salvation based upon the "finished work of Messiah/Christ," does in fact undermine the very basis of true inter-faith efforts at building bridges of understanding.

Believers, when sharing their faith, should have complete freedom to do so, but this must never be based upon the use of deceitful methods, coercion, the offer of personal or material benefits to achieve forced conversions, but by the honest laying out of the facts, demands and cost that a Jewish person will face through a commitment to following Messiah/Christ.

I am reminded of an account given to me in the early 1990's of the Council of Jews, Christians and Moslems, an inter-faith forum that met in Cape Town, South Africa. The Christian and Jewish members spent their time being nice to each other, with the Christians apologizing to the Jewish people for all the things that has been done to them in the "name of Christ," while the Moslems present made no apologies for what they stood for. They simply tried to "convert" the Jewish and Christians members of the council to Islam. So much for this council's efforts at finding a common ground of understanding.

In many respects these types of forums, in not wishing to give offense by seeking the lowest common denominator, are almost a waste of time. Their narrow criteria leave virtually no room to speak truthfully about what is of importance to each faith group represented. Perhaps one of the only positive outcomes from such forums is the fact, that at least, people of different faiths are meeting and speaking with each other.

While I fully understand why Messianic Jews are accused of muddying the waters, I dispute the accusation. As a group or movement of people it is perfectly acceptable for them to develop their own creed and confession of faith as part of their expression of what they believe. This is part of self-identification. This may not be agreeable to those who oppose them from both the Jewish and Christian faith. Yet nonetheless it is their right to give expression to their faith in theologically and culturally appropriate ways, even in the face of the disapproval of others.

A contemporary way of giving expression to oneself as a unique human being is by the use of terms like – self-identity; self-care; self-worth; self-identification and self-awareness. All of these terms are nuanced by different aspects of helping to assert one's independence and worth as a unique individual.

23 — Self-identity

"IF I AM NOT FOR MYSELF, WHO WILL BE FOR ME?" (SELF-CARE)
Rabbi Hillel, a contemporary of
— Yeshua of Nazareth

Ex Jew, Converted Jew, Christian-Jew, Jewish-Christian, Hebrew-Christian, fulfilled Jew, completed Jew, Christian of Jewish heritage, Hebrew Catholic, Jew for Jesus, or Messianic Jew – how should one identify oneself? What should Jewish believers in Jesus be called? It was once explained to me that if someone is referred to as a Hebrew Christian, then that means that person is a Christian of a Hebrew/Jewish heritage. Hebrew is the adjective and Christian is the noun. In contrast a Messianic Jew is a person who is Jewish who believes that Yeshua is the Messiah, yet still considers that they are Jewish. In this case Messianic is the adjective and Jew is the noun. This is not just a question of semantics but is far more significant.

Messianic Jewish identity

There may be those who accuse one of being a terrible person for believing in Yeahua: meshumad – משומד, lit. "destroyed one"; apostate; misfit; crazy; ignorant; disgrace. "Your grandparents would turn in their graves if they knew what you have become!" and "you should be ashamed of yourself!" I have had all of these things said to me and more, over the years. However, there is another way of giving expression to one's personal identity:

> **"If I am not for myself, who will be for me?"**
> (Rav. Hillel)

This begs the question of one's inalienable right to self-identification. While others may attempt to deny one the right to call oneself a Messianic Jew, their attempted negation should be ignored. The way that one chooses to identify oneself is of the utmost importance and is part of self-care. Self-care's primary focus deals with one's physical well-being and health, hygiene, good nutrition, sufficient recreation and sleep. It should also include one's mental health and a sense of inner-harmony and peace.

Who are you and how do you want to be identified?

Those Jewish believers that consistently say that they are Christians have chosen to all but assimilate into the majority Gentile Christian culture. That is their personal liberty but consequently, to all intents and purposes, they are no longer considered to be part of the Jewish people.

In contrast someone who says that they are a Messianic Jew is making a powerful statement. I refer to this as a creative dissonance – though a lack of harmony is sounded by the use of the name of Messianic Jew, causing a lack of agreement or harmony with one's fellow Jews, an opportunity for fruitful dialogue is created. Not only do Jewish people sit up and take note when Messianic Jews bear witness to their identity and faith, equally Christians also want to know what Messianic Jews believe. I constantly have people enquire of me as to what I believe when I say that I am a Messianic Jew.

A conundrum is created when a Messianic Jew claims to be a Jew who believes that Yeshua is the Messiah. Jewish people are very seldom indifferent to this claim, with some becoming hostile and even angry, and occasionally physically violent. I have been on the receiving end of all three types of responses, though only once was I struck in anger and, on another occasion, someone threatened to hit me. However, generally most Jewish people express a genuine interest and I have been able share my faith at great length with some who have asked me to explain myself to them.

The opportunity for Messianic Jewish self-expression has increased exponentially, and it is no longer considered as a movement of disaffected Jewish misfits or Jews who are on the margins of Jewish society and life. There are hundreds of thousands of Messianic Jews throughout the world today. Just as there is a great diversity of how Jewish believers identify themselves, so there are equally numerous types of Messianic Jewish congregations and fellowships. On the one extreme there are Hebrew Protestant and Hebrew Catholic congregations that use the church liturgies and worship songs of those denominations that sponsor them. On the other extreme, there are Messianic congregations that are very similar to Orthodox, Conservative, Reform and Liberal Jewish synagogues and temples. An interesting phenomenon is taking place in modern Israel today with the opportunity of Israelis to give self-expression and self-care to their faith in a distinctively Israeli way. In contrast to Jewish people living in the diaspora who are always a minority, in Israel being a majority Jewish state, Jews feel much more at liberty to explore a more authentically Israeli mode of expressing their faith.

Another example of this greater sense of security is the way that "Israeli Jews have discovered a newfound love with Christmas: 'There is a small Christian minority in Israel, and it's nice that members of the majority (Jewish) are taking the time to familiarise themselves with their symbols and rituals. Jews in the diaspora are always on guard with respect to Christianity and Islam, given their history of either oppressing or converting Jews. But in Israel that dynamic does not exist.'"[65]

This new reality is also having a positive influence with greater openness on the part of Israelis and a willingness to consider the claims of the gospel message about Yeshua's love for Israel. When Jewish people are able to self-identify themselves as Messianic believers, the consequent result is that fellow Jews no longer view believing in Yeshua as something that is alien and foreign to be avoided at all costs. This is a reality that I am able to confirm.

During the period that my wife and I led Beit Ariel Messianic congregation in Cape Town, South Africa (1988-1994), we had many fellow Jews join the congregation. It was a safe place where Jewish people felt welcome to visit and explore the Messianic faith. A Jewish lifestyle was encouraged and most of the Jewish festivals and rituals were observed as well as weekly Shabbat services. These observances included Brit Milah (circumcision), Jewish-style weddings, Bar and Bat Mitzvahs and, at death, Jewish mourning (Sitting Shiva). With this paradigm shift there is much greater freedom to live a Messianic lifestyle before a watching Jewish world. In

Judaism, *halacha* – how we live/walk, is of paramount importance.

In his brilliant book Francis Schaeffer asks, *How Shall We Then Live?* He ponders the fate of declining Western culture. He analyses the reasons for the state of modern society's decline and presents a viable alternative: Living by the Biblical ethic, acceptance of God's revelation and total affirmation of the Bible's morals, values, and meaning. Equally, Yeshua calls believers to be salt and light. Salt preserves and prevents decay and gives flavour to life. Light dispels darkness illumining the pathway preventing stumbling. Just as the prophets of Israel sought to turn people towards God and his ways of righteousness and truth, so Yeshua did the same as the Word made flesh.

Schaeffer says that Yeshua not only points the way, but he is the Way, Truth and the Life. (See John 14:6) This helps to tie together the need for living according to God's pattern and design for Israel and all humankind. For just as God is One, so he has one ethic for all to discern and discover. Though there are numerous interpretations of the outworking of the divine will and purpose, confusion and negative outcomes are due to human failure and the fault does not lie with God's divine revelation.

Bad theological interpretation undermines the foundations of the biblical faith and in the modern era the liberalism that began in the latter part of the 19th century following the Enlightenment became a major contributor to the movement away from orthodoxy. Judaism and Christianity have both suffered as a consequence.

Roni Mechanic

Jews, God and Christian Renewal

Graphic by Roni Mechanic ©

24 — Jews, God and Christian Renewal

Due to their inter-connectedness, Jews and Christians have the same goal and a common destiny in their desire to hasten the coming of the Kingdom of Heaven on earth in the Messianic age of universal peace. Consequently, together they need to strive for the same outcome. To that end, Abraham S Heschel wrote three Essays that address the need for Jewish and Christian renewal. This gives expression to the desire for greater cooperation and joint efforts to bring about the healing of the historic division between our two Abrahamic faiths. This must be pursued with due diligence and determination.

Additionally, with the questions surrounding the dual identity of Jews who are followers of the Jewish Messiah Yeshua, the healing of this division between the two faith is imperative. For just as one grapples with the Jewish understanding about who Yeshua is, so Christians need to have their perception of his Jewishness renewed too.

Though Jews, Christians and Moslems look to Abraham as father, Jewish people continually stumble over the Rock of Offence – Yeshua, Abraham's Greater Son: 1 Peter 2 [8] and 'A stone that makes them stumble, and a rock that makes them fall.'(NRSV)

While Moslems acknowledge Yeshua as a prophet, the Koran and the Hadiths interpret his role in a different way to the New Testament. This discussion is beyond the scope of my book.

In Abraham Heschel's essay – *The Jewish Notion of God and Christian Renewal* (1967), he marks a distinction between the "notion of God" and an "understanding of God," when he says, "The prophets of Israel had no theory or "notion" of God. What they had was an "understanding."

And to paraphrase, according to Heschel, their God-understanding was not the result of a theoretical inquiry, of a groping in the midst of alternatives. To the prophets, God was an overwhelmingly real and shattering present. They never spoke of him from a distance. They lived as witnesses, struck by the words of God, rather than explorers engaged in an effort to ascertain the nature of God. Their utterances were the unloading of a burden, rather than glimpses obtained in the fog of groping.

He continues, "to them the attributes of God were drives, challenges, commandments, rather than timeless notions detached from His Being.[66] "Understanding" can best be explained in this context of Abraham Heschel's discussion about having a knowledge of or familiarity with God, rather than a "notion" of him, i.e., some vague, imperfect conception or idea of him.

In Heschel's vein is a classic by J. I. Packer, *Knowing God*[67] in which Packer echoes Heschel's desire that our experience of knowing God is not based upon some vague notion or an intellectual or head knowledge only. It has to go much deeper and draw us into a communion with God and an experience of prayer. The Psalms encourage us to wait on the Lord even if God appears to keep us waiting. He is not in such a hurry as we are, and it is not his way to give more light on the future than we need for action in the present, or to guide us more than one step at a time. When in doubt, do nothing, but continue to wait on God. When action is needed, light will come.

Packer encourages the reader to turn each truth that we discover about God into a matter for meditation which will also lead us to prayer and praise.

"Knowing God is more than knowing about him; it is a matter of dealing with him as he opens up to you and being dealt with by him as he takes knowledge of you. Knowing about him is a necessary precondition of trusting in him."[68]

This desire of "Knowing God" is a vital part of the human longing. Packer challenges the idea that we can say with compete definiteness that we know God. Our experience of him is not as striking as that.[69]

The longing, as expressed by Dr Packer, resonates with Abraham Heschel's thoughts about the difference between having a "notion" and having an "understanding" of what it means in our desire to know God. The former is a vague inclination, while the latter is motivated by a deeper commitment that both Packer and Heschel express. Heschel shows that to be able to speak adequately about God we would have to know all that God's created beings have been through, both highs and lows from the beginning of time and then we would begin to know how God is relevant to this.[70]

Herschel raises the question of ambiguity. While there are things that have certainty such as the basis of our faith, ambiguity is of value to give us room to manoeuvre within our theological positions. For we face many difficulties and conflicts which face us daily as human beings and things are not cut and dried.

We are not left to ourselves by the God of Israel. Heschel speaks of the darkness that we experience at times in life which God has allowed into our lives. Perhaps these times teach us about the fact that we do not know the secrets of God or understand his ways. Yet we know his name and live by means of his love and grace.

Heschel speaks of the trial that confronts us alongside the certainties of our faith. We have to wrestle with the trial. It builds character qualities into our lives that are necessary to avoid us becoming complacent and passive. If we had no certainty life would be chaotic and it would be as if God was not there for us. Our faith opens us to 'meaning beyond mystery.' Our existence is shaped and modified by faith even if there is fear lest God discard us.

In the angst expressed by Heschel he recalls the words of Job: "Though he slays me, yet will I trust him." (Job 13.15) The image of the broken ladder further illustrates this, "Faith is a high ladder and at times all the rungs seem to have been taken away. Can we replace the rungs? Can we recover the will to rise? And if the rungs cannot be replaced, shall we learn to reach the truth at the top of the ladder?"[71]

25 — "Ambiguity, perplexity, and uncertainty"

From my understanding, words like "ambiguity, perplexity, and uncertainty" may be very awkward and disconcerting for many. Yet they leave an opportunity for the possibility of the true seeker "to reach the truth at the top of the ladder." For the person who desires to reach not only the top of the ladder, but beyond, this has implications to enable Jewish and also Christian enlightenment to take place.

Little Boxes

> Little boxes on the hillside,
> Little boxes made of ticky tacky,
> Little boxes on the hillside,
> Little boxes all the same…

The Malvina Reynolds song made popular by Pete Seeger, "Little Boxes," in its original context addresses the issue of "middle America" and is used to refer to middle class people in the USA who did not to like change and were trapped in living in "little boxes all made out of ticky-tacky and they all looked just the same." In the sixties the social upheaval that shattered their false sense of security in the face of McCarthyism, the Civil Rights movement and the anti-Vietnam War alliance, forced people to break out of those boxes that had trapped them and to break free.

How are we to break free from the stereotypes that we hold about the faith of others, whether Jewish or Christian? This is urgently needed to enable us to stand together against the onslaught that confronts us and that threatens the survival of our two faiths.

Counterculture of the Sixties

Living in South Africa some of the issues that Americans faced due to their cultural upheavals were also experienced and were also having an impact. I personally came under the influence of the counterculture in its manifestation in South Africa. It was felt in Johannesburg, Cape Town and Durban, having an impact upon middle-class young men and women. There was a proliferation of music, films, drugs and sexual liberation that were part of the British and American expression of the counterculture of the 60's.

There was also the struggle against the Apartheid system of oppression and this would become the main focus of a movement that would challenge Apartheid and its oppression and denial of human rights to the majority of South Africans. The USA Black consciousness movement had more of an impact and slogans like "Black is beautiful," gave expression to their growing desire for personal dignity and to shake off the shackles of racial oppression.

One of the consequences of this counterculture was that there was a willingness to challenge the status quo of our parents' generation and their social mores. There was a greater willingness to try out not only new substances such as LSD or marijuana but also new spiritual experiences such as Transcendental Meditation (TM), Hare Krishna, Sufi, San Jasin (Orange People, because of their followers' orange robes) and more importantly the Jesus Freaks (Jesus people) certainly had an appeal.

26 — Jesus Freak

ONE WAY

Jesus Freaks had an impact upon the emerging hippie sub-culture in Johannesburg. I was in the right place at the right time – Johannesburg School of Art and Design. My parents, family and fellow Jews would have said, in the wrong place at the wrong time, because of the consequences that this fresh expression of faith had upon me and a number of other young fellow Jews in Johannesburg.

Johannesburg School of art was one of the places where things began to happen, on two fronts. Sex, drugs, rock and roll (music) and film all played a part in the cultural scene and spiritually there was a growing interest in the occult and also alternative spirituality as offered by people like Rudolf Steiner and his Anthroposophy.

Madam Blavatsky was an occultist, spirit medium, and author who co-founded the Theosophical Society in 1875. She gained an international following as the leading theoretician of Theosophy, the esoteric movement that the Society promoted. She collaborated together Annie Besant (1847-1933), who was a political reformer, women's rights activist, theosophist, and Indian nationalist.[72]

A fellow Art student and friend invited me to a Steiner meeting in Johannesburg and I also visited a theosophical meeting in the city on the advice of another friend in my search for the truth. I perceived greater darkness and not light at these meetings. A mixture of occult and gnostic ideas about being and existence were offered, but no relationship with the living God was spoken of.

A Zeal for God

After having come to faith during my second year of college under the influence of one of my teachers, I went on to become one of the college's unofficial evangelists, proclaiming the Good News at every opportunity.

During my fourth and final year, when we were busy executing our design projects we moved between the design studio and workshops. I entered the studio and second year students were engaged in a design project. One of them turned to me and questioned me about being a Jesus freak? With the lecturer's absence, this gave me the opportunity to proclaim the gospel to the twenty or so students present. I know that at least three or four of those present made a personal profession of faith following that and other encounters.

Jesus' Freaks come to town

During 1969, on our mid-year art college break, a friend and I travelled up to Zimbabwe (still called Rhodesia in those days), and we stayed in Harare (Salisbury) before travelling up to his family farm about 100 miles north of the capital. We were dressed like two hippies as part of that sub-culture of the nineteen sixties. We had shoulder length hair and wore denim jeans. We had hitched hiked a lift from Johannesburg all the way to the neighbouring country of Rhodesia to share our faith with others.

We both carried a handful of gospel tracts that we freely gave to anyone who showed an interest. On entering the famous Miekle's Bookshop in the centre of Harare we offered the proprietor, a Jewish lady, one of our Gospel pamphlets. She took this and we had a most animated conversation with her. At that point she showed us the covers of two of the latest editions of Time magazine – emblazoned on the front cover of one was a photograph of some hippy looking types and the words on the other magazine read, "The Jesus' Revolution." There standing in her shop were two Jesus Freaks. This was the cause of her interest and excitement.

LET YOUR LIGHT SO SHINE
BEFORE ALL THAT THEY MAY SEE
YOUR MITZVOT
AND GLORIFY HASHEM

Roni Mechanic

Time Magazine Jesus' Freak Covers

27 — Jewish and Christian Renewal

For Abraham Heschel his use of the term "renewal" in the context of his 1967 essay, refers to the "movement of Christian renewal," that he sees as "a shift from evasion to confrontation, a willingness to recognise the validity of principles long disparaged or disregarded."[73]

Renewal is a two-edged sword, for the Jewish and Christian faiths both are in need of a reappraisal of where they stand not only in relation to each other, but also in the face of the rapid secularization of the Western world where traditional religious belief is being eroded at an alarming rate.

"Renewal," he says, is not something that takes place only once, "but rather a constant happening," "semper a novo incipere" – "Always from the beginning." It should also be viewed as "a process, not only in relation to others, but above all, one that affects the inner life and substance of the Christian."[74]

Heschel's hope is that Judaism and Christianity will develop in the future towards a profound expression of mutual esteem without denying their disparity and that this will become a means of helping each other in their understanding of their discrete differences and commitments and growth in their cherishing of what God means.

He is clearly concerned in not giving offence in his suggestions as to how Christian renewal can take place. Christian renewal should imply confirmation with Judaism, out of which it emerged. Separated from its source,

Christianity is easily exposed to principles alien to its spirit. The vital challenge for the Church is to decide whether Christianity came to overcome, to abolish, or continue the Jewish way by bringing the God of Abraham and his will to the Gentiles. [75]

Yes, yes!

I fully endorse Abraham Heschel's assertion and one may clearly witness the many aberrant forms of Christianity that have not only departed from its rich Jewish biblical heritage but manifest a total disregard for the principles of love and mutual respect that are enshrined in the teaching of the Torah.

Further, Heschel shows that the battle going on which centres upon the prohibition and suppression of the Hebrew Bible is symptomatic of the multifaceted battle that is taking place and that confronts both Christians and Jews. He used the example of the past suppression of the Bible in the former Soviet Union.[76]

This threat is ongoing in Moslem countries like Saudi Arabia where the possession of a printed copy of the Scriptures is prohibited.

However, with the technological revolution, it is now possible to obtain access to multiple electronic online editions of the Bible in every language in which the Scriptures have been produced. New and old challenges continually emerge that confront the Christian faith, with Marcionism continuing to undermine the way that Christians view their faith. This is particularly the case when New

Testament theological and biblical studies disengage from the context of Judaism, resulting in perpetuating the unresolved tension.

The battle for the Jewish soul of the Christian/Messianic heart of the apostolic faith is of crucial importance. It is not only for those who believe the gospel message, but particularly for Jewish people who may be considering the Messianic claims of the gospel message.

A de-Judaized Christianity offers an unwelcoming place for not only Jewish seekers, but for all who are looking for an authentic Messianic faith. Roots and shoots are an integral part of the one healthy olive tree.

Paul, in Romans 11 (KJV), sounds a strong warning, when he says, [17] "And if some of the branches be broken off, and thou, being a wild olive tree, wert grafted in among them, and with them partakest of the root and fatness of the olive tree;
[18] Boast not against the branches. But if thou boast, thou bearest not the root, but the root thee. [19] Thou wilt say then, The branches were broken off, that I might be grafted in. [20] Well; because of unbelief they were broken off, and thou standest by faith. Be not highminded, but fear: [21] For if God spared not the natural branches, take heed lest he also spare not thee. [22] Behold therefore the goodness and severity of God: on them which fell, severity; but toward thee, goodness, if thou continue in his goodness: otherwise thou also shalt be cut off. [23] And they also, if they abide not still in unbelief, shall be grafted in: for God is able to graft them in again.

[24] For if thou wert cut out of the olive tree which is wild by nature, and wert grafted contrary to nature into a good olive tree: how much more shall these, which be the natural branches, be grafted into their own olive tree? [25] For I would not, brethren, that ye should be ignorant of this mystery, lest ye should be wise in your own conceits; that blindness in part is happened to Israel, until the fulness of the Gentiles be come in.

[26] And so all Israel shall be saved: as it is written, There shall come out of Sion the Deliverer, and shall turn away ungodliness from Jacob:

[27] For this is my covenant unto them, when I shall take away their sins. [28] As concerning the gospel, they are enemies for your sakes: but as touching the election, they are beloved for the father's sakes. [29] For the gifts and calling of God are without repentance…" (KJV)

These are stern words of warning to Gentile believers to not be "high-minded, but fear" God (vs 20), who did not spare the natural Jewish branches of the olive tree.

Christianity without Judaism, is a religion cut off from its roots. Whatever has grown up in place of the true tree, can only be an aberration and its fruit will not have a pleasing, but bitter taste.

Additionally, it is equally very important to note what Abraham Heschel says, that he finds it hard to understand how it is held that the community of Israel was unable to determine the canon of the Hebrew Bible. If this attitude is adopted, then it can equally be argued, then how could the Christian church decide "any legitimacy in the scriptural texts which the New Testament, and Jesus as depicted in it, quoted to authenticate their claim" concerning his place as the Christ/ Messiah and Lord?[77]

Yet again, an anti-Judaism bias led the leaders of the early Christian church who were responsible for determining the canon of Holy Scripture to give expression to their disdain towards the Jewish religion and as said in the opening sentence of the next chapter they were *"plunderers and not partners"* with their Jewish parents who gave them not only the Hebrew Scriptures, but also their blessed Messiah and Lord. Hate instead of love became the touchstone of the emergent Christian church.

Church Triumphant – Synagogue Defeated

Roni Mechanic

Which Edition of the Jewish Scriptures is more valid, the Hebrew or Greek?

𝔐 or LXX?

MASORETIC TEXT OR SEPTUAGINT

Graphic created by Roni Mechanic ©

28 — Hebrew or Greek translation of the Bible?

*

Making our personal response

Plunderers and not partners, is an apt description of a Christian church, that instead of honouring its parents, has robbed it of all that is sacred to it by appropriating all its blessings and leaving only the curses for Israel.

"The standard Hebrew Bible is called the Masoretic Text (MT or 𝔐) and is the authoritative Hebrew and Aramaic text of the Tanakh (Hebrew Bible) for Rabbinic Judaism. It was primarily copied, edited and distributed by a group of Jews known as the Masoretes between the 7th and 10th centuries C.E. [78]

The majority of the New Testament quotations and references are generally taken from the Septuagint or LXX. In Latin Septuagint literally means "seventy." It is sometimes called the Greek Old Testament and is the earliest extant Greek translation of the Old Testament from the original Hebrew. It is estimated that the first five books of the Old Testament, known as the Torah or Pentateuch, were translated in the mid-3rd century B.C.E. and the remaining texts were translated in the 2nd century B.C.E.

Under Christian auspices, the Septuagint includes the Hebrew Bible as well as the deuterocanonical books of the Christian Old Testament. Considered the primary Greek translation of the Old Testament, it is quoted a number of times in the New Testament, in Pauline epistles, by the Apostolic Fathers, and later by the Greek Church Fathers. [79] Many of these quotations are older than the Masoretic text and offer a different slant to it when quoted in the New Testament.

*

HINENI

'Here I am" – HINENI; Hier bin Ich' :

וַאֹמַר, הִנְנִי שְׁלָחֵנִי.

Those who attempt to discredit or undermine the Hebrew Bible, are effectively being like someone who wants to keep the tree growing and healthy but disparages the roots of the tree and therefore digs up the tree and separates the branches from its root stock. Then they wonder why the tree withers and dies. A New Testament expression of faith severed from its Hebraic roots will face the same fate as the tree in my illustration. Christianity without Judaism will die, having no other option open to it.

Abraham Heschel expands upon this by asking a rhetorical question: "Why is the Hebrew Bible indispensable to our existence? It is because the Bible urges us to ask and listen: What does God require of me? It is through the Bible that I learn to say, "Here I am!"

This expression "Here I am!" is discussed in Franz Rosenzweig's "The Divine Call" in his book *Star of Redemption*: As humans are the object of this divine love, when God makes a direct call, "Love me now," (Lieb mich Heute), what is the response? "As in the call of Abraham in

Genesis 22.1, we see the first genuine example of a divine-human dialogue in Scripture, 'Here I am' (HINENI, Hier bin Ich). (Rosenzweig, p. 158)

In Genesis 1, we read the story of God with Adam and Eve. The relationship between them develops from the naming of Adam which the Hebrew indicates as Ha-Adam which is 'the human' to his wife Eve who is named in Hebrew as Ha-Ishah or the 'the wife.'

There is a progression in Genesis 2 and 3 as the humans are becoming personalities. We read of God's loving care for them and his guidance in their life in the garden. They have tasks to perform and one prohibition regarding the tree in the midst of the garden which they are not to eat from or even touch. When they disobey God's instructions and he calls them they hide from him. Obedience always goes hand in hand with the call of God.

Returning to Abraham, there is the double call, "Abraham, Abraham." Then and only then can a human respond, "Here, I am" – (HINENI).

Moses made his response to the Self-Revealing-God at the Burning Bush in Exodus 3:4:

[4] When the Lord saw that he had turned aside to see, God called to him out of the bush, "Moses, Moses!" And he said, "Here I am."

When God speaks, many of us are like people in a fog and we give no answer. Moses' reply to God revealed that he knew where he was and that he was ready. Readiness means having a right relationship to God and having the knowledge of where we are. We are so busy telling God where we would like to go. Yet the man or woman who is ready for God and his work is the one who receives the prize when the summons comes. We wait with the idea that some great opportunity or something sensational will be coming our way, and when it does come, we are quick to cry out, "Here I am."

Hearing the call of God means that we are prepared to do what he wants us to do however small or large it may be. We listen in obedience to God's nudging and are ready to do what he plans for us. We trust that God will lead us forward even if the pathway ahead is not very clear to us. We are ready to do his calling because we love him and want to follow him even as the Lord heard his Father's voice and followed him throughout his life and ministry.

We need to be ready for God may take us by surprise. Taking a time with God each day will help us to be ready for him when he calls us. Moses saw the burning bush in the midst of the desert and he perceived that the presence of God was near him, for the bush was not consumed by fire. He heard the voice of God and he was willing to say yes to God.

Once more in Isaiah 6, the prophet makes his response to God:

[6]In the year that King Uzziah died, I saw the Lord sitting on a throne, high and lofty; and the hem of his robe filled the temple. [2]Seraphs were in attendance above him; each had six wings: with two they covered their faces, and with two they covered their feet, and with two they flew. [3]And one called to another and said: "Holy, holy, holy is the LORD of hosts; the whole earth is full of his glory." [4]The pivots on the

thresholds shook at the voices of those who called, and the house filled with smoke.

⁵And I said: "Woe is me! I am lost, for I am a man of unclean lips, and I live among a people of unclean lips; yet my eyes have seen the King, the LORD of hosts!" ⁶Then one of the seraphs flew to me, holding a live coal that had been taken from the altar with a pair of tongs. ⁷The seraph touched my mouth with it and said: "Now that this has touched your lips, your guilt has departed and your sin is blotted out." ⁸Then I heard the voice of the Lord saying, "Whom shall I send, and who will go for us?" And I said, "Here am I; send me!" ⁹And he said, "Go and say to this people:" (NRSV).

When the Bible urges us to ask and listen, this is not to ask some nebulous or empty question, but those deep and profound issues of the meaning of our existence and being. The call to Israel given in the "Shema" – "Hear O Israel" is about the divine call and while it is addressed in its original context to Israel, it applies to all who are willing to "listen" to what the Scripture says, in both the Hebrew Bible and the New Testament.

"The place and power of the Hebrew Bible is so important, because all subsequent manifestations of doctrines, whether in Judaism or Christianity derive their truth from it, and unless they are continually judged and purified by it, tend to obscure and distort the living relationship of God to the world."[80]

Abraham Heschel's concern is that because the Bible is largely missing from our contemporary culture, its power does not judge the life of our world in the lifegiving way in which it should. The Bible is there but it does not speak in a vacuum. He compares the Bible to a sledgehammer which requires an anvil such as the prophets were as they cried out with the words of God and pleaded with the people.

Heschel speaks of the words of God as being like gates which open and shut with possibilities of engagement with God and like the notes and chords of music clearly sounding out and yet concealing his presence. He sees the roots of our contemporary nihilism which is the age-old resistance to the Hebrew Bible and its people. The power of the Bible shatters the illusion that we can be innocent bystanders in the world.

Innocent bystander

This question of one being an innocent bystander is particularly pertinent in the light of my having been born in South Africa during the dark days of the Apartheid regime. The Nationalist government that inaugurated Apartheid rose to power in 1948, the year of my birth. Their justification for racial segregation was motivated by the desire to maintain white domination.

White only Apartheid Signs
29 — Apartheid South Africa: 1948–1994:

Living in Apartheid South Africa

I am reminded that when living in Apartheid South Africa we faced many challenges:

With our discussion about the call of God, personally, as well as collectively, living and growing up in an Apartheid society, making my own response, "HINENI," became increasingly important.

What are the roots of Apartheid?

South Africa's roots are in the Dutch and British colonial past that favoured the European settlers and discriminated against the indigenous people – the Khoikhoi (Hottentots) and San people (Bushmen) and came into conflict with the Bantu-speaking tribes that had migrated from North-East Africa and met the Settlers in Natal and the Eastern Cape. The principal tribes were the Zulus in Natal and the Xhosas in the Eastern Cape. The immigration and migration of these diverse people, alas, bore within it the seeds of conflict.

"The word 'kaffir' was originally used by Arab slavers to denote unbelievers or heathens. It came to be used in nineteenth-century South Africa to refer to any Bantu, particularly a member of the Xhosa tribe. In the 20th Century the term Kaffir became a slur, and eventually politically incorrect. Its use today as a pejorative term constitutes hate-speech.

The Kaffir Wars, also referred to as the Xhosa Wars and the Cape Frontier Wars, were a series of conflicts from 1779 to 1879 the precise number of which is uncertain but generally counted as nine, fought along the eastern border of the Cape Colony between settlers of Dutch and British origin and the Xhosa people.

Also known as 'Africa's 100 Years War', these different conflicts were a series of flare-ups in one long war of attrition – the longest in the history of colonialism in Africa. These Kaffir Wars are distinguished by the unwillingness of the colonial rulers, Dutch or British, to side with the Boers (Afrikaners), and they made repeated attempts to prevent fighting by setting up borders and lands that were off-limits to settlers.

In 1948, under the Apartheid regime, racism became institutionalised, and its racial theories were strengthened by Nazi's ideas about race. Dr H.F. Verwoerd, a Hollander, who had been a member of the Hitler Youth in Holland during the era of the Nazi occupation, brought to South Africa the racial theories that he had learnt while still in the Netherlands. Verwoerd is referred to as the "High Priest of Apartheid." Apartheid Law that applied to Black South Africans was promulgated during the oppressive years under the Nationalist ruling party from 1948–1994.

As stated, the concept of "Separate Development," was meant in theory to be separate, but equal. But, in reality, a very different situation took place. For example, 90% of the education budget was spent on the white population of six million whites which made up only 20% of the total population. Because of forced separation between the white population and all other ethnic groups, the Prohibition of Mixed Marriages Act forbade any racial mixing in order to preserve the white race. Apartheid proved to be an odious political ideology and, in many ways, it was as bad as Nazism.

All South Africans were held prisoner by it, oppressor and the oppressed alike were not free, due to a spiritually and morally bankrupt evil ideology.

The divide and rule axiom became the norm and persisted and led to the development of the concept of separate development, forming the basis of Apartheid that became enshrined as a political ideology to maintain the white minority's dominance. Whites enjoyed all the privileges of living in an unequal society while the rest of the South African population – black, Coloured (mixed race) and Asian – were treated as second-class citizens and suffered deprivation to varying degrees. It was meant to be separate and equal, but the harsh reality was very different as this political system was enforced on the majority of the non-white population that were disenfranchised and had little, if anything, to say about those things that governed their daily lives. How humiliating and dehumanising to be described as a "non-person." In contrast the "Black Pride" and slogans such as "Black is beautiful" help to redress some of the use of racially demeaning words.

Apartheid bus sign indicating racial segregation

All forms of racial prejudice and racial stereotyping must be resisted by all peaceful means and instead of building barriers of fear and suspicion, bridges of love and acceptance should be our common pursuit and goal.

Black, Jew, Arab, Gypsy, Rohingya, First-Nation (Native American Indian), Inuit (Eskimos), Hispanic, Yazidi, Mawari Bheels – and other Dalits (India, Pakistan, Bangladesh and Sri Lanka), Khoikhoi (Hottentots), San People (Bushmen) and others. This list is by no means exhaustive as there are many other groups that suffer prejudice and exclusion and need to be included, such as women, children, gays, trans-sexual, people with disability, etc. Each deserve to be shown dignity and respect.

South Africa's Jewish Population

Just as the Black population of South Africa was denied basic human rights, so too South Africa's substantial Jewish population had to struggle for full civil, religious and human rights. In 1903 with the arrival of Russian and Eastern European Jews severe restrictions were placed on these new arrivals,

"Granted that none of these movements (i.e. those Jewish communal groups such as the Jewish Board of Deputies and the South African Zionist Federation), have fully justified the hopes set on them, still are they not as many proofs that the number of South African Jews is growing who hold that as long as one of us is not free, we are none of us free? This sentiment contains within itself the possibilities of a better future. With God's help and our best efforts, the better future will be ours." (Inaugural Public Meeting of the Jewish Board of Deputies of the Transvaal and Natal – (Herman), 1905/ reprint 2018). [81] This statement "as long as one of us is not free, we are none of us free," is a truism that applies to all of South Africans whatever their racial, religious or cultural origins.

In a Jewish context, the Jewish people had suffered under racial and religious prejudice for nearly two millennia and faced their worst experience of race-hatred under the Nazis, beginning in the nineteen-thirties, and culminating with the Holocaust that ended with the conclusion of WWII. In 1948 when Israel achieved statehood, she finally realised her dream of self-determination and a national homeland for the Jewish people. The phrase "Am Yisrael Chai" – The People of Israel Live! equally affirms the Jewish right to live and be masters of their own destiny in their own land.

While the main focus of racial discrimination was directed at people of colour, Jews did not escape a certain amount of anti-Semitism, and this occurred particularly during the Nazi era due to the fact that South Africa was honeycombed with pro-Nazi cells. Though the main focus was anti-British, the Jewish people were not unscathed by anti-Semitic and race-hate propaganda.

In the present post-Apartheid South Africa, Jewish people are being targeted by certain factions within the government ANC party and the opposition EFF, due to South Africa taking a strong pro-Palestinian and anti-Israel stance, and now accusing Israel of being an Apartheid state. Though many leading Jewish politicians and industrialists during the Apartheid era did positively promote black people in business and the arts, however, because Israel and the South African Nationalist government were in a military alliance with Israel being a major arms supplier, Israel remains unforgiven for aiding the South African repressive regime. Life is complex!

While I was at primary school in Johannesburg, on the curriculum was the odious subject of 'Race Studies'. The prescribed textbook had illustrations of the ethnographic racial stereotypes of African sculls and faces. Those who designed these books sought to prove that the brains and physical structure of Africans were of more primitive human beings. These vile and repulsive images have left a lasting impression that was imprinted upon my young mind. Even at that young of age of 10 – 11 years old, I recall feeling distinctly uncomfortable with those racial theories. Suddenly one day our class teacher collected all the textbooks and the subject disappeared from the curriculum.

Attempts to use Scientific Racism to justify Apartheid surely had elements of the Nazi racial theories and its attempt to establish the idea of the master race and to prove that the Aryan/Nordic racial type was superior to the Jewish, Gypsy, and Slavic types. The German term Herrenvolk, "master race" was used in 19th century discourse that justified colonialism with the racial superiority of Europeans. This was based not only on bad science, but also gave them justification in their programme of dehumanisation of inferior races and resulted in the slave trade. For the Nazis it ultimately led to destruction and deliberate annihilation in one of the ghastliest acts of genocide during the Holocaust that humankind has ever witnessed.

Though the Apartheid system and ideology lacked a final solution to the black problem, many of the outcomes bore a resemblance to what happened in Nazi Germany. Separation and exclusion; pass laws; restricted labour laws assigning black people to doing only menial tasks; forced removals; police brutality; and political assassinations are some of the more obvious factors that constituted the Apartheid system.

Hold my head in shame

Unless we actively opposed that evil racial discrimination of the Apartheid world, we were complicit and I look back in shame as a privileged white that, though I disapproved, I did not take a more active stand against that morally reprehensible system. To use Abraham Heschel's words, there are "no innocent bystanders" and this is equally true of Apartheid. What does this say to all who witness desperate acts of discrimination and cruelty wherever they take place, and yet keep silent? Though there were many who were appalled by the Apartheid system, the majority of white South Africans kept the Nationalist government in power for over forty years.

Our guilty silence

First, They Came For The Jews – Poem by Martin Niemöller

First, they came for the Jews
and I did not speak out
because I was not a Jew.

Then they came for the Communists
and I did not speak out
because I was not a Communist.

Then they came for the trade unionists
and I did not speak out
because I was not a trade unionist.

Then they came for me
and there was no one left
to speak out for me. [82]

Let us not live under any illusions

As Nelson Mandela said, hating another, just as loving someone, is something that people must learn to do. "For love comes more naturally to the human heart than its opposite." Both Judaism and Christianity stress the importance of showing love and forgiveness to one's enemies. Also, it is equally important to show compassion and to care for those who are vulnerable and on the margins of society, for they need to be treated with respect and human dignity.

We read in Deuteronomy 10:19 (NIV) "And
you are to love those who are foreigners, for you yourselves were foreigners in Egypt."

In Ephesians 4.32, OJB puts it this way, "And have Chen v'Chesed – graciousness with one another. Be kind, tender hearted, forgiving each other, as also Hashem in Rebbe, Melech HaMoshiach (GOD, in Rabbi King Messiah) forgave you."

NIV translation renders it: "Be kind and compassionate to one another, forgiving each other, just as in Christ God forgave you." Putting aside all desire for revenge towards those who have done us wrong, forgiveness is the touchstone of all who seek to love God and their fellow human beings.

Photo by Roni Mechanic ©

No one is born hating another person
because of the color of his skin,
or his background, or his religion.
People must learn to hate,
and if they can learn to hate,
they can be taught to love,
for love comes more naturally
to the human heart than its opposite.

July 18, 1918 - December 5, 2013 *Nelson Mandela*

Nelson Mandela

30 — Redeemer Revealed, Judge and Creator

For Abraham Heschel, God is not only Redeemer and Revealer, but he is also Judge and Creator as well. His contention is that when people are detached from the Hebrew Bible, they begin to cherish one perspective of the meaning of God. In the case of Christians, they prefer His promise as Redeemer.

Heschel writes of God's demanding presence as Judge and his transcendence as Creator. Many people tend to speak of his love, and they neglect the fact of God's judgement and wrath. Stress is placed in theology on the immanence of God as we think of his nearness and loving care and forget that he is also the transcendent God. Stressing one side such as his miracles and that he is there for us while ignoring the mystery of God is a dangerous distortion.[83]

A Different Perspective

Heschel makes a plea not to neglect the Hebrew Bible which will result in an unbalanced perspective on the person and character of the God of Israel. While this plea not to neglect the Sacred Scriptures is sound, however, in the context of his argument concerning who the God of Israel is, he is in danger of presenting a caricature of those who hold to a different perspective based upon sound New Testament Biblical theology. His contention may hold true for some, yet it certainly is not the case for all who uphold the New Testament interpretation of the person and character of God. An Orthodox Jewish interpretation always denies that Yeshua is the divine Son of God and thereby remains true to Jewish orthodoxy. However, I seek to hold in balance God's imminence and transcendence, recognising that there is a difference in interpretation. For on the one hand God shows loving-kindness and mercy, as for example expressed in the Psalms, while on the other hand we must contend with the reality that God is also Judge and King and may seem to be absent.

Franz Rosenzweig says that miracles demonstrate God's imminence versus "the infinite darkness of His absence" (transcendence). This is given witness to in the Psalms, Job and the Prophets. From a New Testament perspective, the cry of utter desolation of Jesus upon the cross, with the words in Mark 15:33-39 (cf. Psalm 22.2), affirms Rosenzweig's contention that at times God's absence is stark.

Where was God in the darkness?

The sense of the presence of God is not always obvious, particularly when darkness envelops life.

On a number of occasions when people that I have met are confronted with tragedy and loss with the suffering and death of a loved one, or when they personally may be confronted with great difficulties, they have asked: "Where is the God of love that you have spoken of?"

Yeshua faced great darkness

Mark 15:34 (NRSV), [33]When it was noon, darkness came over the whole land until three in the afternoon. [34]At three o'clock Jesus cried out with a loud voice, "Eloi, Eloi, lema sabachthani?" which means, "My God, my God, why have you forsaken me? (cf. Psalm 22:1)

אֵלִי אֵלִי, לָמָה עֲזַבְתָּנִי

Similarly, C.S. Lewis in *A Grief Observed*, speaks of the utter darkness, as he was confronted with the death of his, wife, Joy Gresham Lewis:

"You can't see anything properly while your eyes are blurred with tears. You can't, in most things, get what you want if you want it too desperately: anyway, you can't get the best out of it. The time when there is nothing at all in your soul except a cry for help may be just the time when God can't give it: you are like the drowning man who can't be helped because he clutches and grabs. Perhaps your own reiterated cries deafen you to the voice you hoped to hear." [84]

St. John of the Cross writes in his poem, *The Dark Night of the Soul*, "We must discuss the method of leading the three faculties (intellect, memory, and will) into this spiritual night, the means of divine union. But we must first explain how the theological virtues, faith, hope, and charity… through which the soul is united with God, cause the same emptiness and darkness in their respective faculties: faith in the intellect, hope in the order in the memory, and charity in the will. Then we shall explain how in order to journey to God the intellect must be perfected in the darkness of faith, the memory in the emptiness of hope, and the will in the nakedness and absence of every affection."[85]

Roni Mechanic

This darkness or blackness can also be interpreted as entering "the Cloud of Unknowing," and this is in order for us to enter into a deeper union and subsequent communion with God.

This description of the spiritual journey is not unique to the Christian, but, as Abraham Heschel describes, the Jewish seeker equally will experience the desire to "cleave to God," as in the concept of "kavanah" כַּוָּנָה in Biblical Hebrew, literally meaning "intention" or "sincere feeling, direction of the heart." It is the mindset often described as necessary for Jewish rituals – *mitzvot* – מִצְווֹת means observing the commandments and prayers "tefilla" תְּפִלָּה.

The light did shine in the darkness and the light of God overcame the darkness. Daylight follows a dark moonless night, but how much more does the light of God overcome spiritual blackness in the human soul. Each one of us are called to turn towards the eternal light of God. [86]

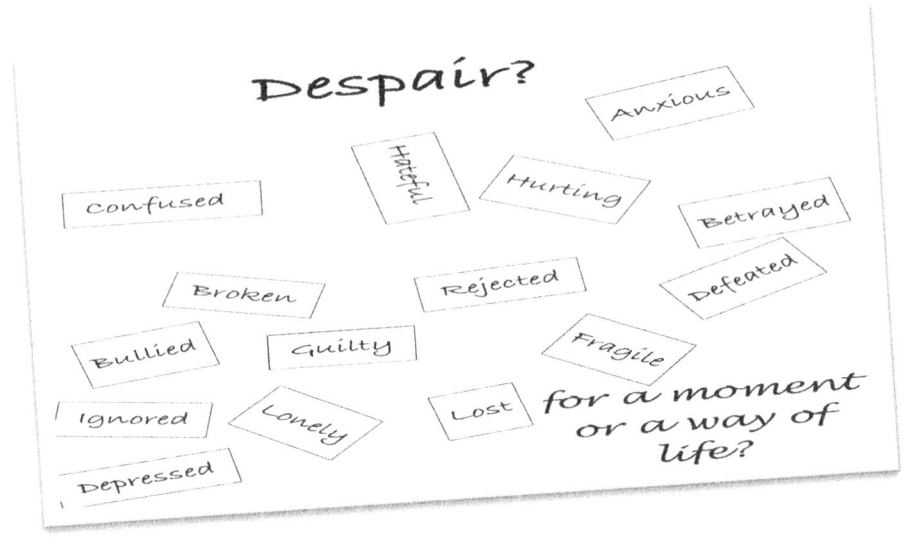

Graphic created by Roni Mechanic ©

31 — Despair for a moment or a way of life?

Well, is despair a way of life or is it something that we can break out of? The human condition is, in reality, a constant struggle against meaninglessness as expressed by an existentialist pessimism such as in Franz Kafka's books *The Castle* and *The Trial* or his book *Metamorphosis*. In response to this rather depressing and fatalistic worldview, Martin Buber turns to the work of Emil Brunner, a Modern Christian theologian. In his book *Mediator*, Brunner explores the Pauline view of God in which there is a hope of redemption in the face of hopelessness: Paul's cry of desolation: "O wretched man that I am! Who shall deliver me from this body of death?" (Romans 7.24, King James Version – KJV).

While Martin Buber did not share Emil Brunner's faith in Christ, yet he drew encouragement from his outlook. The human condition is not simply a continual struggle against meaninglessness for there is an alternative to despair to be discovered. "I thank God through Jesus Christ our Lord. So then with the mind I myself serve the law of God; but with the flesh the law of sin." (Romans 7.25, King James Version – KJV).

The Castle, and The Trial

An analysis by Fritz Rothschild in 'Jewish Perspectives on Christianity,' helps explore the work of the Jewish poet Franz Kafka's novels *The Castle*, and *The Trial*, in which there are a number of powerful similes that reflect our age.[87]

The Castle, originally written in German: – Das Schloss/ Das Schloß is a 1926 novel by the Jewish author Franz Kafka, who lived and worked in the Bohemian city of Prague, a centre of rich Jewish cultural life. It is a story about a protagonist known only as K. who arrives in a village and struggles to gain access to the mysterious authorities who govern it from a castle. Kafka died before finishing the work but suggested it would end with K. dying in the village, the castle notifying him on his death bed that his "legal claim to live in the village was not valid, yet, taking certain auxiliary circumstances into account, he was permitted to live and work there." Dark and at times surreal, *The Castle* is often about alienation, and unresponsive bureaucracy, with the frustration of trying to conduct business with non-transparent, seemingly arbitrary controlling systems, and the futile pursuit of an unobtainable goal.

The Theological Outlook of Kafka

Max Brod, was born on 27 May, 1884, in Prague, Bohemia, Austria-Hungary, now called the Czech Republic. He died on 20 December 1968, in Tel Aviv, Israel. He was a German novelist and essayist known primarily as the friend of Franz Kafka and as the editor of his major works, which were published after Kafka's death. It is well documented by Max Brod that Kafka's original construction of *The Castle*, was based on religious themes. Numerous interpretations have been made with a variety of theological angles.

One interpretation of K.'s struggle to contact the castle is that it represents a man's search for salvation. According to Mark Harman, translator of a recent edition of *The Castle*, this was the interpretation favoured by the original translators Willa Muir and held by Edwin, who produced the first English edition in 1930. A biblical interpretation of the novel is strongly supported because there are various names and situations derived from Holy Scriptures. For example, an official is called Galater. This is the German word for Galatians, one of the initial regions to develop a strong Christian following from the ministry of the Apostle Paul and his companion Barnabas. The messenger in the Castle also bears the name Barnabas.

By naming the beginning chapter "Arrival" suggests that K. is compared to an Old Testament messianic figure, whose mission is obstructed by the vested interests of those who wish to maintain the status quo. Similarly, the second chapter is called "Barnabas." This strong biblical imagery pervades and is spread throughout the novel, subtly building the narrative. Another example is the choice of the term "Land surveyor," in German Mashoah, being almost the same as Mashiah, which is the Hebrew word for Messiah.

Martin Buber gave expression to a more joyous form of Judaism through Chasidic spirituality. Buber shows that a law-based authoritarian world that is rigid and lacking in a basic humanity is mirrored by the dystopian world in Kafka's works. These include *Metamorphosis*, *The Castle*, and this is equally true of his novel *The Trial*, where there is a random, senselessness that unfolds in the Kafkaesque world, having a nightmarishly complex, bizarre or illogical quality, where all the characters are caught up in bureaucratic senseless delays. Those trapped in that world truly face an existential conundrum that appears to have no way out because it is almost completely devoid of saving grace. Yet there is the occasional glimmer of hope portrayed in some of Kafka's characters. This faint "hope" with an element of human kindness and compassion is evidenced in some of the characters in *The Castle*.

However, in *The Trial*, K.'s life ends with him being stabbed through the heart. It does not appear that due process was followed by the judges or councillors who presided over his trial. K.'s defence layer suggested that the best outcome that he could hope for is endless postponements in the unlikely event of an acquittal. There does not appear to be any rhyme or reason given as to what K. is even guilty of. Nonetheless, he is put to death at the end with no explanation given other than assumed guilt for some imagined or unnamed crime. The prison chaplain offers no hope either when he says to K. that the law is not a door of hope and its way is closed to K. who is shown no mercy or grace through it, but only judgement and his ultimate death.

The three torturous scenarios played out in Kafka's principal novels, are actually only one scenario with three different settings. However, each situation shows glimmers of compassion and hope shown to the victims of the impossible situations that they find themselves in. Yet in each case there is the existentialist resignation to their helplessness. According to the existentialist philosophy, life is just like that, and there is little if anything that one can do to alter one's destiny.

Judaism, while not a fatalistic religion as is Islam, does prescribe that the way to achieve a fruitful godly and fulfilled life is to follow the way of the mitzvot (commandments) as recorded in Deuteronomy 28. Consequently, it should go well with one and this will result in not only a long life, but a fulfilled and blessed one too. Kafka's writing tries to make sense of a world that is perplexing and his search, as a nonreligious Jewish person, reflects a deep pessimism and uncertainty, though he is not totally without hope.

As you may recall Kafka's writing was presented to me during my late teens by one of my Habonim leaders. Lee flax introduced me to the existential outlook that characterised secular thinking back in the 1960's among young Jewish intellectuals in Johannesburg.

In my personal quest this spurred me on to discover a pathway to finding hope and meaning which I chose, and not the way of despair which was but for a moment!

Mayim Chaim — מים חיים

I remember at a Habonim summer camp that took place in the beautiful eastern Cape town Onrus on the coast. One evening we sat around a campfire and sang songs led by someone playing a guitar and also someone on a piano accordion. One of the song's lyrics has stayed with me till this day. 'Jesus met the woman at the well and told her everything she had ever done..." This was based on the gospel narrative of Yeshua's encounter with the Samaritan woman at Sychar: John 4.4-15 (NIV), [4] Now he had to go through Samaria. [5] So he came to a town in Samaria called Sychar, near the plot of ground Jacob had given to his son Joseph. [6] Jacob's well was there, and Jesus, tired as he was from the journey, sat down by the well. It was about noon. [7] When a Samaritan woman came to draw water, Jesus said to her, "Will you give me a drink?" [8] (His disciples had gone into the town to buy food.) [9] The Samaritan woman said to him, "You are a Jew and I am a Samaritan woman. How can you ask me for a drink?" (For Jews do not associate with Samaritans). [10] Jesus answered her, "If you knew the gift of God and who it is that asks you for a drink, you would have asked him and he would have given you living water." [11] "Sir," the woman said, "you have nothing to draw with and the well is deep. Where can you get this living water? [12] Are you greater than our father Jacob, who gave us the well and drank from it himself, as did also his sons and his livestock?" [13] Jesus answered, "Everyone who drinks this water will be thirsty again, [14] but whoever drinks the water I give them will never thirst. Indeed, the water I give them will become in them a spring of water welling up to eternal life." [15] The woman said to him, "Sir, give me this water so that I won't get thirsty and have to keep coming here to draw water."

What on earth were we doing?

How was it possible that a group of Jewish teenage youngsters at a Habonim summer camp should be singing a powerful gospel song? Did we sing it because it was a popular folk ballad or was there a deeper reason that one of our leaders had chosen this song for us to sing? I will never know the answer to that question, but one thing is clear that I personally longed to drink from the living water! In Hebrew the words "mayim chaim" – מים חיים, literally mean 'living waters' or 'a well of water springing up into everlasting life.' We should note that the Hebrew word for water is in the plural form, designating well or a spring, such as the well that Jacob's servants dug. (Gen. 26:19) This is not just water to quench human thirst, but a deep well-spring of spiritual life-giving water that is opened to all those who turn to Yeshua the 'Living Water.' Jews and Gentiles alike are welcomed by God who extends his mercy to all.

Victor Frankel: Logo Therapist

Victor Frankel, the famous Holocaust survivor and Logo Therapist (The Viennese Third School of Logo Therapy, founder), wrote an excellent book called, *Man's Quest For Meaning*. His basic thesis is that without meaning, the alternative is depression and despair. He found, through his personal experience of surviving the Auschwitz concentration camp, that to have a reason to live can help cure many forms of deep clinical depression. As he put it – what makes you want to get out of bed in the morning? His school of therapy has helped countless people overcome the sense of purposelessness and meaninglessness by finding a reason to live.

Though separated from his beloved wife while in the death camp, he held onto the memory of his love for her and he said that this hope sustained him. He did not know that she had died, yet nonetheless his pure love of her gave him a reason for hope and this aided his survival despite the dreadful deprivation of Auschwitz. He recalled that another fellow inmate, a Baptist Christian, was also helped not to despair due to his belief in God. Even in the darkest places, the flame of hope can be kept alight through having a focus to live for. A living faith does aid mental health and recovery from metal and psychological illness, as well as assisting a greater sense of personal wellbeing.

The choices that we can make

Not everything that happens to us as human beings is as a result of the choices that we make. Yet, when bad things happen, we can make the choice as to how we respond. Though the universe is broken, we do not live in a random and chaotic universe. Nonetheless, we are able to make our personal response to what happens. This is well illustrated in the way that Victor Frankel responded to the most extreme depravity of the Nazi regime

"On this day, we gather because we have chosen hope over fear." These words of optimism were said by Barack Hussein Obama from the Capitol, with that symbol of democratic freedom and power as a backdrop. His message of hope was delivered after taking the oath of office as the 44th president of the United States. Obama's message of hope is equally needed today as when he spoke then.[88]

Not only is Donald Trump's America a more fractured and polarised place since Obama gave that speech but our world today, in 2020, is an even more damaged place as we face the Covid-19 pandemic. We are confronted with a choice of either giving into despair or choosing to hope. "I call heaven and earth to record this day against you, *that* I have set before you life and death, blessing and cursing: therefore, choose life, that both thou and thy seed may live:" (Deuteronomy 30.19 - KJV).

32 — Modernity and post-modernity[89]

With modernity one is presented with certainty and life is predictable up to a certain point. Purpose, principles, faith and a framework of predictability are some of the things that characterise how things should work. On the other hand, post-modernity is characterised by uncertainty and random things happening. Deconstructionist, dysfunctional and dystopian is the world in which we live.

This post-modernity is reflected in art, literature, theatre and film. There are no happy endings. Good does not necessarily triumph over evil and no one lives happily ever after.

Another aspect of post-modernity is a sense of foreboding and impending disaster, resulting in an apocalyptic cataclysm in which life as we know it will end. This is particularly reflected in a number of films such as *Independence Day*; *The Day After Tomorrow*; *The Twelve Monkeys*; *Deep Impact*; *The Road*; *The Children of Men*; *Elysium*; *Cloud Atlas and the Book of Eli*. This list is by no means exhaustive.

Most of these films reflect upon a world either after a nuclear war or some other cataclysmic disaster that was caused by climate change. In each film there has been a global catastrophe with few survivors. Or the end of life on earth as we knew it took place due to a chemical/viral attack that wiped out most of life on the planet's surface as in *The Twelve Monkeys*. *The Book of Eli* stands out as the one film in the post-apocalyptic genre where a glimmer of light shines with the rediscovery of the King James Bible. This is the one book that offers hope in an otherwise desolate world.

These threats and portents of disaster are not new and have been a feature of Jewish and Christian apocalyptic for eons. Even at the time of Yeshua's earthly life there was a strong tradition of Jewish apocalyptic literature and in that age, the Jewish hope was for divine intervention. Yeshua's own disciples question him on a number of occasions as to whether the end of the age was about to happen:

MATTHEW 24 (KJV):
[1] "And Jesus went out and departed from the temple: and his disciples came to him for to shew him the buildings of the temple. [2] And Jesus said unto them, See ye not all these things? verily I say unto you, There shall not be left here one stone upon another, that shall not be thrown down. [3] And as he sat upon the mount of Olives, the disciples came unto him privately, saying, Tell us, when shall these things be? and what shall be the sign of thy coming, and of the end of the world?

[4] And Jesus answered and said unto them, Take heed that no man deceive you. [5] For many shall come in my name, saying, I am Christ; and shall deceive many. [6] And ye shall hear of wars and rumours of wars: see that ye be not troubled: for all these things must come to pass, but the end is not yet. [7] For nation shall rise against nation, and kingdom against kingdom: and there shall be famines, and pestilences, and earthquakes, in divers' places."

As I have shown, these portents of impending suffering and judgement have not only spawned a whole genre in the film industry but, equally, many of these films were based on a great swathe of apocalyptic genre Christian and secular literature. Religious writings have also influenced the arts with religious paintings by people like Michael Angelo and Albert Durer to mention just two who have depicted the coming apocalypse and judgement graphically.

Judgement without redemption is a very frightening prospect. However, according to the Scriptures, humankind is always offered an opportunity to turn away from wrongdoing and turn towards a loving and forgiving God. This is not only true according to the New Testament's teaching, but the Hebrew Scriptures repeatedly show how God extends grace to all.

The Prophets of Israel

Both Biblical and extra-biblical (non-canonical writings) foretell and warn of judgement leading to, not only national, but also individual suffering because of human wickedness and disregard for moral ethical righteousness and a failure to honour God and our fellow human beings. Idolatry and turning away from serving the living God are just some of the causes for the "wrath to come" upon the unrepentant and godless behaviour of kings, rulers and even people in religious authority. Israel, because of its covenant relationship, is a particular focus for the prophets but also the other nations will be judged for wickedness and idolatry.

The Prophet Amos is a good example of someone who proclaimed that judgment day was coming:

Roni Mechanic

Amos 1 [2] "And he said, The LORD will roar from Zion, and utter his voice from Jerusalem; and the habitations of the shepherds shall mourn, and the top of Carmel shall wither. [3] Thus saith the LORD; For three transgressions of Damascus, and for four, I will not turn away the punishment thereof; because they have threshed Gilead with threshing instruments of iron: [4] "But I will send a fire into the house of Hazael, which shall devour the palaces of Benhadad. (KJV)

"For three transgressions …, and for four" – this means that the full measure of wrongdoing will be judged – "3 + 4 = 7" which is the divine number of completeness. God was completely fed up and all other options had run out!

These salutary words are given by the writer of Ecclesiastes 3 when he says, "And moreover I saw under the sun the place of judgment, that wickedness was there; and the place of righteousness, that iniquity was there. [17] I said in mine heart, God shall judge the righteous and the wicked: for there is a time there for every purpose and for every work." (KJV)

May we apply our hearts and minds to pursue the wisdom of God so that in all our doings we might find divine favour and not be brought to a place of reckoning and the consequent judgment. May we discover God's favour and blessings in this world and the next.

33 — The Holy Yehudi - Yeshua

A pressing concern exists when considering Buber's presentation of 'the holy Yehudi.'

Isaiah 49 [2] He made my mouth like a sharp sword, in the shadow of his hand he hid me; he made me a polished arrow, in his quiver he hid me away.

Buber's believed that Jesus is one among many luminaries found within the tradition of Hassidic messianism, for he is surely a great man, but he is nothing more than that. Yet he is inconsistent because he is willing to concede that for Gentiles Jesus is God and Saviour.

Break out and break free

We all face choices and we can choose to remain captive to fear and ultimately a death filled with despair as Kafka's 'K.' faced in *The Trial*, or we can choose life with purposeful meaning.

The Messianic faith does not only give a way out, but also a promise of a brighter future. This is not an illusionary "pie-in-the-sky-when-you-die" future or "the opiate of the people" according to Karl Marx. Belief and faith in God and his Messiah are not an escapism from the harsh reality of life or, as someone said, a crutch to lean on but is the gate of hope in this life and in the world to come.

Yeshua wept over Jerusalem,

[37] O Jerusalem, Jerusalem, thou that killest the prophets, and stonest them which are sent unto thee, how often would I have gathered thy children together, even as a hen gathereth her chickens under her wings, and ye would not! (Matthew 23:37 (KJV)

Yes indeed, how much more can we hope for?

Tears of sorrow will be turned to peals of laughter and singing when Israel shall look upon the "pierced one," and recognise him as their own. Not only will he be recognised, but Yeshua will embrace her with open arms. May that day hasten and soon dawn. The forgiving, reconciling nature of God is yet to be fully recognised by Israel and the nations. Not a Kafkaesque dystopian world but a future filled with the hope of life fulfilled in God's kingdom, through his Messiah, Yeshua. The Holy Scriptures are filled with many promises that God will restore the fortunes of Zion, with Zion being a symbol of the Jewish nation. There is a two-fold restoration promised, namely the Kingdom of God and the Son of Man.

The theology of Rudolf Otto

Among the late nineteenth and early twentieth century German theological thinkers and writers, Rudolf Otto stands out as a most important person. He who wrote a number of significant books. In *The Idea of the Holy* Otto explores the concept of the numinous and the supernatural.

The word numinous is from the Latin 'numen', meaning 'divine will' or 'nod' that suggests a figurative nodding of assent or of command of the divine head. In English the use 'numen' carries the meaning 'a spiritual force or influence' and can refer to those who are endowing it with several senses: 'supernatural' or 'mysterious.' It may also convey the idea of someone who is "possessed by a numinous energy force." It can also mean the 'holy' or "the numinous atmosphere of the catacombs" and other places where a holy or numinous sense is felt. This can particularly be the case in places of worship or to coin a contemporary phrase a 'scared space or place'. [90]

God showed up

I have on a number of occasions experienced over the past forty years a sense of the 'other' or the 'holy', and to use Rudolf Otto's language, one witnesses what are a number of extra-ordinary sensory phenomena:

For Otto, the numinous can be understood to be the experience of a mysterious terror * and awe, and majesty in the presence of that which is 'an entirely other' and thus incapable of being expressed directly through human language and other media. *(mysterium tremendum – "mystery that repels," in which the dreadful, fearful, and overwhelming aspect of the numinous appears) —
https://www.britannica.com/topic/mysterium-tremendum-et-fascinans

During a twelve-year period (2001–2013) I taught Contemporary Judaism as an elective course at the Nazarene Theological College, Manchester University, to third year under-graduate students. On an appointed pre-arranged day, we attended a day of teaching that I conducted together with one of the synagogue elders at Altringham Orthodox Congregation, Manchester.

Roni Mechanic

In the morning session the elder explained synagogue worship with my group of twelve students. After a short lunch break, we moved to a side teaching room and chapel in the synagogue building.

I spread a large tallit (prayer shawl) over the table around which we were seated. Our discussion for the afternoon session was Jewish scared texts, which included the *Pirkei Avot* – <u>Hebrew</u>: פִּרְקֵי אָבוֹת; which translates in English as *Chapters of the Fathers* or *Ethics of the Fathers*. It is a compilation of the ethical teachings and maxims passed down to the Rabbis, beginning with Moses and onwards. It is part of the Mishnaic tractate of Avot and is unique in that it is the only tractate of the Mishnah dealing solely with ethical and moral principles.

Following our consideration of the *Pirkei Avot*, we turned out attention to the Amidah. This is a moving example of Jewish prayer where the worshiper moves from praise to petition and then to thanksgiving. The Amidah inculcates a sense of connection to God.[91]

Though the house (the room in the synagogue) did not literally shake, we were nonetheless enveloped with an awesome sense of the presence of the 'Holy Other'. This was the best way to describe what we all felt – 'God showed up!' As commented above, when one has a sense of the numinous, one is incapable of being able to directly express through human language what we experienced.

Another most influential book by Rudolf Otto is, *The Kingdom of God and the Son of Man*. He describes his understanding of the Kingdom of God to be the heavenly realm where God's will is done, the supra-historical sphere where God rules. Jesus' teaching is grounded in a dualism of earth vs. heaven. The heavenly realm is a 'wholly other' existence, and Jesus announced the coming of this miraculous, supernatural realm.

This event is exclusively God's deed and will mean the breaking off of history and the descent of the heavenly realm to earth. The Kingdom of heaven will come down from above and effect a marvellous transformation of the world.

The Lord's Prayer is a petition for the coming of this supernatural, heavenly realm. However, Jesus believed that the Kingdom was already in the process of coming. This he believed because in a vision he had seen Satan overthrown in heaven. (Luke 10:18) Therefore, he knew that God had already achieved victory over Satan and that the Kingdom had already been realised in heaven. A tidal wave of divine victory had been set up by virtue of which the powers of the Kingdom of God were already operative on earth.

This is what Rudolf Otto means by his oft-quoted statement, "It is not Jesus who brings the kingdom... the kingdom brings him with it."[92] "The future heavenly realm is already breaking into the world through Jesus in the form of a wonderful, supernatural, coercive power operating from above. The Kingdom is not only the eschatological realm; it is also victorious, coercive power. The eschatological realm of salvation is already breaking into the world as a divine *dynamis* – (the state of that which is not yet fully realised as in power or potential). In the future age Jesus will become the heavenly Son of Man; but he is already the agent of the present in-breaking power of the Kingdom."[93]

This recognition has helped recent biblical scholarship to avoid the earlier pitfall of relegating the role of the Hebrew Scriptures to that of mere preparation or precursor for the Gospel. One cannot escape the fact that for the Jews of the Hebrew Scriptures, salvation was not an abstract concept, but a real and present experience.

Martin Buber had tremendous difficulty with the New Testament declaration that in Jesus the Kingdom of God had come, when clearly all around one witness anything but the universal peace that the dawning of the messianic age is meant to bring. Ladd, Otto, Schweitzer and many other theologians have attempted to explain the apparent contradiction in the Christian declaration that the Kingdom of God has come with the Advent of Jesus.

An Aliyah

34 — An Aliyah

I visit the Western Wall each time I am in Israel and in 2018, I went to the Kotel on the last day of Pesach (Passover) and stood facing those ancient stones and experienced that sense of connection and destiny that each Jew has when he or she stands in the place of contemplation and prayer.

On the Shabbat (Sabbath) there are numerous groups of Jewish men praying around bemas (prayer desks) gathered in front of the wall on which Torah scrolls are placed with the designated Torah portion being read. A group of orthodox men invited me to share an "Aliyah" (literally meaning "to go up") and read from the Torah scroll placed on their prayer desk.

What Does It Mean to Have Faith?

The Torah reading on that particular morning described Israel's experiences following the exodus. Pharaoh mobilises the Egyptian army and begins his pursuit of the fleeing Israelites. When Moses and the children of Israel reach the Red Sea, Moses raises his rod, the waters split apart, and the Israelites are miraculously saved. When the Egyptians reach the water, they become bogged down, sink to the bottom, and are drowned. Moses and the children of Israel sing a magnificent song of thanksgiving. They faced two options, despair or having faith in God to deliver them?

For many Israelites this imperative to "Go Out" was a step forward in their learning to trust in God to be their Deliverer instead of giving into fear. Another way to express this is having an active thrusting faith in the Living LORD.

On my completion of this Aliyah, I experienced a profound sense of elation having had the privilege of participating in the reading of the Torah at Judaism's most holy site, standing in front of the Western Wall of the Temple. Going up (Aliyah) and Going out (Beshalach), express something of the sentiment of what I, together with a multitude of fellow Jews, have sought to achieve. There is movement and activity that takes place throughout this book.

"According to Jewish tradition no other prophetic revelation would surpass this miraculous event. Emil Fackenheim similarly calls the divine deliverance from Egypt through the waters of the sea, as well as the revelation at Sinai later, Israel's two "root experiences."[94]

According to Christian tradition, their most significant revelation is the coming of Emmanuel, God-with-us, in the person and work of Yeshua HaMashiach/Jesus the Messiah.

Having explored the purpose and procedure of participating in an Aliyah, I wish to consider the significance of a reading from 2 Chronicles 36:

[22] In the first year of King Cyrus of Persia, in fulfilment of the word of the LORD spoken by Jeremiah, the LORD stirred up the spirit of King Cyrus of Persia so that he sent a herald throughout all his kingdom and also declared in a written edict:

[23] "Thus says King Cyrus of Persia: The LORD, the God of heaven, has given me all the kingdoms of the earth, and he has charged me to build him a house at Jerusalem, which is in Judah. Whoever is among you of all his people, may the LORD his God be with him! Let him go up (literally to make Aliyah)."

We should also note that 2 Chronicles is the last book in the Hebrew Bible according to the order of the Masoretic text 𝔐 of Sacred Scriptures. In contrast the last book in the Greek Septuagint (LXX) order of the books of the OT ends with these words from Malachi that declares a curse. This is the order of the Christian Bible.

A blessing with going up to the Land of Israel in the 𝔐 (MT), while a curse in the LXX – one may wonder why this book is the choice in the completion of the Old Testament in the Christian cannon?

Abraham Heschel concludes with these poignant words,

"The words have gone out from here and have entered the pages of holy books. And yet Jerusalem has not given herself away. There is much more in store. Jerusalem is never at the end of the road. She is the city where the expectation of God was born, where the anticipation of lasting peace came into being. Jerusalem is waiting for the prologue for the new beginning."

"What is the secret of Jerusalem? Her past is a prelude. Her power is in reviving. Her silence is prediction: the walls are in suspense. It may happen any moment: a shoot may come forth from the stump of Jesse; a branch may grow out of his roots." (Isaiah 11.1) [95] – (Rothschild, 1990:340)

Roni Mechanic

Shalliachim – Emissaries of Reconciliation

The word Beshalach means "to go out" and is related to another Hebrew word Shalliach (Hebrew: שליח, pl. שליחים/שלוחים) which speaks of those who are emissaries and ambassadors, and in a New Testament context signifies apostolic preachers and pioneer missionaries.

The Apostle Paul says,
2 Corinthians 5:20 (NRSV)
[20] So we are ambassadors for Christ, since God is making his appeal through us; we entreat you on behalf of Christ, be reconciled to God.

2 Corinthians 5:20 Complete Jewish Bible (CJB),
[20] Therefore we are ambassadors (Shalliachim, pl. - שלוחים) of the Messiah; in effect, God is making his appeal through us. What we do is appeal on behalf of the Messiah, "Be reconciled to God!

The implication of this in the light of the Parasha Beshalach is to go out as Shalliachim (pl.) - שלוחים and that we are being called to respond by encouraging others to not only be reconciled to God, but to each other. I wish to underscore this desire in fostering a greater Jewish-Christian understanding of each other's faith.

Becoming emissaries of inter-faith bridge building we must recognise that there is yet much more to be achieved for this to take place. This should not dissuade us from endeavouring to undertake this vital work of healing reconciliation between the two faiths. However, we need to recognise those issues that divide us – the primary issue being the question of who Yeshua is, and what he came to do. The divinity question is the biggest cause of disagreement and division. Even his miracle working, healing ministry are not a major stumbling block for Jewish people, but the claim that he is the divine Son of God – Emmanuel, that is the difficulty.

A new optimism

While historically a wide gulf has existed between Judaism and Christianity, due to a multitude of issues dividing the two faith over the last two millennia, there are significant and positive changes that are taking place. Though progress is often with fits and starts, there is considerable scope for a new optimism.

My attempt has been to reclaim Yeshua/Jesus from a distorted image to his true Jewish identity and heritage. There are a number of significant factors that are contributing to this change that is taking place. From a Jewish perspective what began to happen during the 19th century saw a new willingness for Jewish scholars to begin to reclaim Jesus as one of their own. Christian attitudes were also changing in their perception of Judaism. Consequently, Jewish and Christians scholars were willing to begin a sincere dialogue, with a new openness to each other.

Another factor has now come into play due to the significant number of Jewish believers who are no longer totally disregarded as renegades, apostates and marginalised former-Jews. Generally Messianic Jews are not seriously considered by most of their fellow Jews to be really Jewish, and many are quick to assert that Messianic Judaism is merely Christianity dressed in Jewish garb. Yet there are growing numbers of Jewish scholars and rabbinic voices who are willing to consider the possibility that Yeshua believing Jews are no longer totally beyond the pale. The Messianic Jewish movement is growing steadily throughout the world.

A New Interpretation of Synagogue and Church – Together as Equals and Partners

35 — Last words

However, my work is not yet done, for I have loose ends to tie together in my quest for the Jewish Jesus. We are left with an "opening of hope" - פֶּתַח תִּקְוָה - Petah Tikva.

And with not only an opening of hope, but also with the anticipation of the dawning of the Messianic age when Jesse's greater Son will come to his own people, in the city of the great King David, Yeshua HaMashiach.

Jewish hope and Christian/Messianic longing are tied together with a united anticipation and a common destiny. For just as Jerusalem stands as the symbol of Jewish expectation, so too, for the Christian/Messianic believer, the return of Yeshua to Jerusalem is promised in Acts 1.6-11: [6]So when they had come together, they asked him, "Lord, is this the time when you will restore the kingdom to Israel?" [7]He replied, "It is not for you to know the times or periods that the Father has set by his own authority. [8]But you will receive power when the Holy Spirit has come upon you; and you will be my witnesses in Jerusalem, in all Judea and Samaria, and to the ends of the earth." [9]When he had said this, as they were watching, he was lifted up, and a cloud took him out of their sight.[10]While he was going and they were gazing up toward heaven, suddenly two men in white robes stood by them. [11]They said, "Men of Galilee, why do you stand looking up toward heaven? This Jesus, who has been taken up from you into heaven, will come in the same way as you saw him go into heaven." (NRSV)

What are the implications of these words, "This Jesus, who has been taken up from you into heaven, will come in the same way as you saw him go into heaven?" Abraham Heschel, together with many other Jewish and Christian thinkers said, "It may happen any moment, …"[96] This is clear thinking and that leaves little open to speculation.

While Jewish people say that this will be the first coming of the Messiah, for Christians there is no hesitation to their hope of his return. We share a common beginning and we will most certainly be united in our common end.

Many having read my book may feel that they want to know more about Yeshua, but I encourage you not only to increase your understanding, but to personally encounter him too.

From a Jewish perspective

Jewish people are looking at Yeshua and are reading the New Testament having made considerable progress from the days when to even say his name was anathema and also to pick up a copy of the New Testament that was considered a book of lies and curses. Today it is being reclaimed as a "Jewish classic piece of literature" that is not only being read, but also the New Testament claims are being carefully considered. While different conclusions are being made, none-the-less it is now an open book whose pages are no longer forbidden or sealed to Jewish people.

He is the Jewish Jesus. He came that we may have life and that means an abundance of God's blessing in this life and the gift of eternal life is bestowed upon all who believe. He is not just a Jewish Jesus; he is Messiah and Lord

A Quest for The Jewish Jesus

Jewish & Christian Perspectives

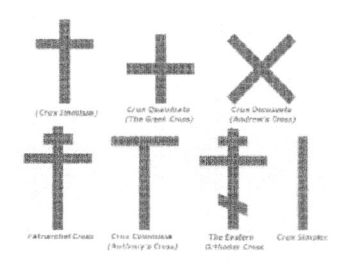

*

The End

Roni Mechanic

A Heart's Desire

Come, my Way, my Truth, my Life :
Such a Way, as gives us breath :
Such a Truth, as ends all strife :
And such a Life, as killeth death.

Come, my Light, my Feast, my Strength :
Such a Light, as shows a feast :
Such a Feast, as mends in length :
Such a Strength, as makes his guest.

Come, my Joy, my Love, my Heart :
Such a Joy, as none can move :
Such a Love, as none can part :
Such a Heart, as joys in love.

(George Herbert)

A Quest for The Jewish Jesus

Cohen's (Priest's) Blessing

*

Num. 6:24-26

יְבָרֶכְךָ יְהוָה וְיִשְׁמְרֶךָ׃
יָאֵר יְהוָה פָּנָיו אֵלֶיךָ וִיחֻנֶּךָּ׃
יִשָּׂא יְהוָה פָּנָיו אֵלֶיךָ וְיָשֵׂם
לְךָ שָׁלוֹם׃

Aaronic Blessing
(with transliteration)

Roni Mechanic

[May] Adonai bless you, and guard you –

יְבָרֶכְךָ יהוה, וְיִשְׁמְרֶךָ

(*Yevhārēkh-khā Adhōnāy veyishmerēkhā* ...)

[May] Adonai make His face shine unto you, and be gracious to you –

יָאֵר יהוה פָּנָיו אֵלֶיךָ, וִיחֻנֶּךָ

("*Yā'ēr Adhōnāy pānāw ēlekhā vihunnékkā* ...)

[May] Adonai lift up His face unto you, and give to you peace –

יִשָּׂא יהוה פָּנָיו אֵלֶיךָ, וְיָשֵׂם לְךָ שָׁלוֹם

("*Yissā Adhōnāy pānāw ēlekhā viyāsēm lekhā shālōm.*")

36 — Bibliography

- Allen, Jonathan, 2018, A Profile of Jewish Believers in the UK Church, USA: Wipf and Stock Publishers
- Baeck, Leo, 1949, The Essence of Judaism, USA: Schocken Books, Revised Edition
- Baker, Leonard, 1980, Days of Sorrow And Pain, Leo Baeck and the Jews of Berlin, New York, USA: Oxford University Press
- Boteach, S, Kosher Jesus, 2012, Israel: HaGefen Books,
- Brower, K. E., 1997, The Reader Must Understand, Leicester, England: Apollos
- Buber, Martin, 2004, Two Types of Faith, New York, United States: Syracuse University Press,
- Buber, Martin, 1970, I and Thou, Translated by Walter Kaufmann, Edinburgh, UK: T&T Clark
- Brunner, Emil, 2018, Mediator, India: Facsimile Publisher, (Reprint)
- Buksbazen, Lydia, 1955, They Looked for a City, NY, USA: Friends of Israel Gospel Ministry,
- Bultmann, Rudolf, 1996, Existence of Faith, Shorter Writings, United Kingdom: Hodder & Stoughton
- Burchill, Julie, 2019, "Fresh 'N' Funky Anti-Semitism," UK: The Sunday Telegraph, (Sunday 3 February)
- Chambers, Oswald, 1935, My Utmost For His Highest, USA: Dodd, Mead & Co.,
- Cohen, Lenard, 2018, The Flame, Edinburgh, UK: Faggen, R & Pleshoyano, A, Canongate

- Cohn-Sherbok, Dan, 2001, Voices Of Messianic Judaism, Baltimore, USA: Lederer Books
- Dimont, Max, Jews, 1962, God And History, New York, USA: Simon And Schuster
- Davies, W D, 1970, Paul and Rabbinic Judaism: Some Rabbinic Elements in Pauline Theology, London: SPCK,
- Douglas, Mary, 1966, Purity and Danger, London, UK: Routledge Classics
- Eckstein, Yechiel, 1984, What Christians Should Know About Jews and Judaism, Texas, USA: Word Books,
- Edersheim, Alfred, 1971, The Life and Times of Jesus the Messiah, USA: Eerdmans,
- Faggen, R & Pleshoyano, A, 2018, Leonard Cohen, UK: Edenborough,
- Flew, Anthony, 2007, There Is ~~No~~ A God, England: Harper Collins,
- Flusser, David, 1997, Jesus, Jerusalem, Israel:
- Fruchtenbaum, Arnold G., 1983, Hebrew Christianity, Its Theology, History, & Philosophy, California, USA: Ariel Ministries Press,
- Gandhi, M. K., 1927, An Autobiography Or The Story Of My Experiments With Truth, Ahmeddabad, India, New Haven and London: Yale University Press.
- Gane, Roy E., 2017, Old Testament Law For Christians, USA: Baker Publishing
- Gill, Robin, 1985, A Textbook Of Christian Ethics, Edinburgh, UK: T&T Clark,

- Gobel, Phil, 2010, The Orthodox Jewish Bible, AFI International Publisher, Bible Institute, New York, USA
- Goldberg, Louis, 2011, Our Jewish friends, Chicargo, USA: Moody
- Goldberg, Louis, 1992, Are there two ways of atonement? Confronting the controversies, Lederer Publications, Baltimore, USA
- Golding, Louis, 1938, The Jewish Problem, Hammersmith, England: Penguin Books,
- Gray, John, 2018 Seven Types of Atheism, England: Allen Lane,
- Green, Michael, 1970, Evangelism in the Early Church, London: England, Hodder & Stoughton
- Guinness, Os, 2016, Impossible People, Oxford, England: Inter-Varsity Press
- Hagner, Donald, 1984: The Jewish Reclamation of Jesus, USA: Zondervan Publishing Company
- Harries, Richard, 2003, After Evil, Oxford, England: Oxford University Press
- Harris-Shapiro, Carol, 1999, Messianic Judaism, A Rabbi's Journey Through Religious Change In America, Boston, USA: Beacon Press
- Hebrew University, Magnes Press
- Herford, R Travers, 1903, Christianity in Talmud & Midrash, London: UK, Williams & Norgate
- Hertz, Joseph H. (Joseph Herman), 1905, , The Jew in South Africa, Milton Keynes UK: Biblolife, (Reprint 2018)
- Herberg, Will, 1955, Protestant, Catholic, Jew, USA: University Of Chicago Press; (Reprinted Ed edition - 1983)

- Herberg, Will, 1951, Judaism And Modern Man – An Interpretation of Jewish Religion, USA: Stefan Salter,
- Heschel, Abraham J., 1997, Between God And Man, An Interpretation of Judaism, New York, USA: Free Press Paperbacks,
- Heschel, Abraham, J, 1999, Man Is Not Alone; God in Search of Man; Harris-Shapiro, Carol, Messianic Judaism, A Rabbi's Journey Through Religious Change In America, Boston, USA: Beacon Press,
- Heschel, Abraham Joshua, 1951, Man Is Not Alone, A Philosophy of Religion, New York, USA: Farrar, Straus, and Giroux,
- Heschel, Abraham Joshua, 2018, God In Search Of Man, London, England: Souvenir Press
- Heschel, Susannah, Abraham Geiger and the Jewish Jesus, 1998, USA: University of Chicago Press
- Heschel Susannah, 2008, The Aryan Jesus, USA: Hendrickson Publishers,
- Hodges, H.A., 2018, Wilhelm Dilthey (1944), Reprint: Delhi, India: Gyan Books Pvt. Ltd.
- Houlden, Leslie, 1991, Judaism and Christianity, London, UK: Routledge
- Kac, Arthur W., 1980, The Messiahship of Jesus, Grand Rapids, USA: Baker Books,
- Kafka, Franz, 2014, The Essential Kafka, England, Wordsworth Edition,
- Kavanaugh, Kieran, 2010, The Collected Works of St John of the Cross, U.S.A: ICS Publications, (Rev ed. edition 31 Dec. 1979)
- Klein, Charlotte, 1975, Anti-Judaism In Christian Theology, London, England: SPCK,

- Ladd, George, 1996, THE PRESENCE OF THE FUTURE, USA: Eerdmans
- Lapide, Pinchas, 1984, The Resurrection of Jesus, UK: SPCK Publishing
- Lieu, Judith M, 1992, The Jews Among Pagans And Christians, London, England: Routledge,
- Lieu, Judith M, 2002, Neither Jew nor Greek, London: T & T Clarke,
- Lochery, Neill, 2004, Why Blame Israel, England: Icon Books
- Maimonides, Moses, 1952, The Guide of the Perplexed, Cambridge, England: Hackett Publishing Company
- Margonet, Jonathan, 2008, Forms of Prayer: Daily, Sabbath and Occasional Prayers, Reform Judaism Prayer Book, London, UK: The Movement for Reform Judaism
- Niebuhr, Reinhold, 1949, Faith and History, London, UK: Nisbet & Co.
- Niemöller, Martin, 1939, Pastor Niemöller And His Creed, London: Hodder & Stoughton,
- Otto, Rudolf, 1923, The Idea of the Holy, London, England,: Oxford University Press,
- Packer, J.I., 1988, Knowing God, England: Hodder & Stoughton,
- Putman, Hilary, 2002, Jewish Philosophy As A Guide To Life, USA: Indiana University Press,
- Rosenzweig, Franz, 2005, Star of Redemption, USA, The University of Wisconsin Press, USA: (English edition 1912)

- Rothschild, Fritz, 1990, Jewish Perspectives on Christianity, New York, USA: Crossroad Publishing Company
- Sacks, Jonathan, 2007, The Authorised Daily Prayer Book, London, UK: Collins,.
- Sacks, Jonathan, 2015, Not In God's Name, London, England, Hodder & Stoughton,
- Samuelson , Norbert M, 1999, A User's Guide to Franz Rosenzweig's Star of Redemption, Surrey, UK: Curzon Press,.
- Sanders, E. P., 1981, Jewish And Christian Self-Definition, Volume II, Philadelphia: Fortress Press,
- Schäfer, Peter, Judeophobia, 1943, USA: Harvard University Press,
- Schonfield, Hugh J., 1936, The History of Jewish Christianity, London, England: Duckworth
- Sharon, Gustav & Hotz, Louis, 1955, The Jews in South Africa, A History, Cape Town, RSA, George Cumberlege, London: Oxford University Press
- Solomon, Norman, 1996, A Short Introduction To Judaism, Oxford, UK: Oxford University Press,
- Stern, David, H., 1979, The Jewish New Testament, Jerusalem, Israel: The Jewish New Testament Publications,
- Stern, David, 1992, Jewish New Testament Commentary, Jerusalem, Israel: The Jewish New Testament Publications
- Stern, David, 1998, The Complete Jewish Study Bible, USA: Hendrickson Marketing

- Stern, David, 1988, Messianic Jewish Manifesto, Jerusalem, Israel: The Jewish New Testament Publications
- Tolkien, J. R. R. 1971, The Lord Of The Rings, Great Britain: Book Club Association.
- Vermes, Geza, 2003, Jesus in His Jewish Context, UK: SCM Press,
- Von Harnack, Adolf, 1902, "What is Christianity? London: Williams and Norgate,
- Witherington III, Ben, 1997, The Jesus Quest, USA: Inter-Varsity Press
- Wenham, Gordon, 2000, Story As Torah, Grand Rapids, USA: Baker Academic Books,
- Vidal-Naquet, Pierre, 1996, The Jews, History, Memory And The Present, New York, USA: Columbia University Press

37 — Glossary of Terminology

AKA — Also known as
BBC — The British Broadcasting Corporation
B.C.E. — Before the Common Era
BDS — The Boycott, Divestment and Sanctions Movement against Israel
C. — Century
C.E. — Common Era – while Christians choose A.D. from the Latin expression "Anno Domini" – "the Year of Our Lord." It refers to the years which followed the birth of Jesus Christ.
CND — The Campaign for Nuclear Disarmament
Jo'burg — Johannesburg
L-rd — Out of Jewish deference for Lord the o is substituted with a – (hyphen)
LORD — YHWH or Tetragrammaton; Adonai or HaShem —The Name
LXX — Septuagint is the Greek translation of the Hebrew Bible
MT or 𝔐 — Masoretic Text of the Hebrew Scriptures (OT)
NTC — Nazarene Theological College
NT — New Testament or New Covenant Scriptures
OT — Old Testament or Hebrew Bible or Hebrew Scriptures
pl. — plural
PMPY — Push Me Pull You
RM — Roni Mechanic
Shema – Hear O Israel
THE INSTITUTE — THE INSTITUTE for the
Study and Eradication of Jewish Influence on German Church Life
Tenach/Tanach – Hebrew for Hebrew Scriptures; also referred to as the Old Testament by Christians
TM — Transcendental Meditation
UK — United Kingdom
USA — United States of America
WWI — World War One or Great War
WWII — Second World War

ABOUT THE AUTHOR

Roni Mechanic is an artist, theological educator, writer, conference speaker and Messianic Jew. He has studied theology up to Master's degree level. Roni taught Contemporary Judaism at the Nazarene Theological College, Manchester University, UK. This is also where Roni was awarded his MA in Theology, 2000.

In addition, Roni is involved in inter-faith dialogue, particularly Jewish-Christian relations, and also Moslem and Israeli-Palestinian bridge-building. Recently, Roni participated in a Holocaust Remembrance Day Inter-Faith service at which he gave the main address:

https://hotrodronisblog.com/2019/01/29/yom-hashoah-holocaust-remembrance-day-27-01-2019-interfaith-service-co-durham/

Roni is married to Elisheva and they have three grown up children and four grandchildren. They live in the United Kingdom.

Contact: mtmi.teaching@gmail.com

✱

Roni Mechanic

Learn more about Judaism and Messianic Jewish perspectives by listening to Shalom Radio UK:

www.hotrodronisblog.com

Graphic by Roni Mechanic ©

Shalom Radio UK

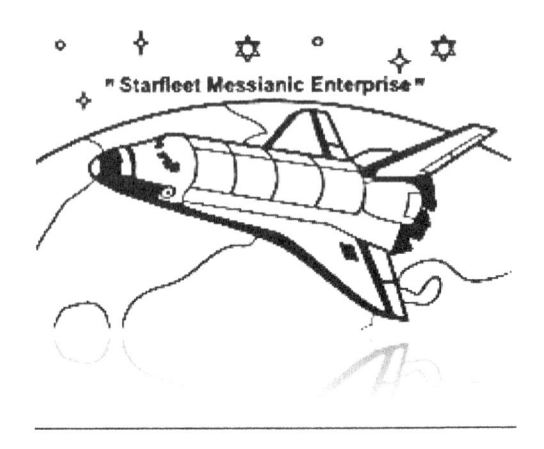

A Quest for The Jewish Jesus

End Notes

[1] *Push-Me-Pull-You* - is a sports game for 2–4 players who are joined at the waist, you and your partner share a single worm-like body as you wrestle your opponent for control of the ball - It's a bit like a big hug, or playing soccer with your small intestines. With every action affecting both you and your partner (and mandatory shouting) PMPY combines the best parts of co-op multiplayer with the worst parts of your last breakup. https://pmpygame.com

[2] See www.uscatholic.org/articles/201608/was-jesus...

[3] Ben-Chorin, Shalom, *The Image of Jesus in Modern Judaism*, Journal of Ecumenical Studies 11, no. 3 – Summer 1974:408; also see p. 26

[4] Sharon, Gustav & Hotz, Louis; *The Jews in South Africa, A History*; 1955:381

[5] https://www.hebcal,com/holidays/shabbat-shuva

[6] Ethan Bronner, https://shalom.kiwi/2016/02/5-broken-cameras-a-distorted-lens/

[7] https://www.independent.co.uk/news/uk/home-news/labour-antisemitism-jewish-hate-incidents-cst-jeremy-corbyn-israel-crime-abuse-a8766551.html

[8] http://www.myjli.com/survival/index.php/2017/03/19/anti-zionismanti-semitism-new-face-on-an-old-hate/

[9] https://www.facebook.com/campaignagainstantisemitism/

[10] To once again quote Rabbi Dr. Leo Baeck (Rothschild, 1990:26; also see page 3)

[11] Heschel, S, *The Aryan Jesus* 2008:26

[12] http://www.religionfacts.com/rudolph-bultmann

[13] Heschel, S, *The Aryan Jesus* 2008:26

[14] Bultmann, R, *Existence of Faith, Shorter Writings*, 1961:217

[15] *loc. cit.*

[16] Heschel, S, *The Aryan Jesus* 2008:28

[17] ibid pg.33

[18] Bethge, Eberhard, *Dietrich Bonhoeffer*, 1970, A Biography, Collins, London, UK; pg 207

[19] Witherington III, Ben: *The Jesus Quest*: Inter-Varsity Press, US; 1997:9

[20] Rothschild, 1990:303

[21] Heschel S, *Abraham Geiger and the Jewish Jesus*, 1998:11

[22] https://hotrodronisblog.com/2016/11/08/shalom-radio/

[23] https://www.goodreads.com/book/show/13293552-kosher-jesus (Boteach, S; *Kosher Jesus*, Israel; Gefen Books; 2012)

[24] Rothschild, 1990:303-304

[25] https://www.encyclopedia.com/environment/encyclopedias-almanacs-transcripts-and-maps/rites-passage-jewish-rites

[26] https://www.chabad.org/

[27] Vermes, Geza, 2003, *Jesus in His Jewish Context*, SCM Press; pg 2

[28] https://www.merriam-webster.com/dictionary/Heilsgeschichte

[29] Lapide, Pinchas, *The Resurrection of Jesus*, SPCK Publishing; 1984:44

[30] ibid pg. 45

[31] ibid pgs. 45-46

[32] ibid pg. 46
[33] Tolkien, J. R. R. *The Lord Of The Rings*, 1971, Book Club Association, Great Britain - from the film script
[34] *The Lord Of The Rings* - Ankit Sachan Published on 29 Aug 2008 – https://www.youtube.com/watch?v=IOmtjCfuRvc
[35] Heschel S, *Abraham Geiger and the Jewish Jesus*, 1998:127
[36] hotrodronisblog.com
[37] Stern, David H.; Jewish New Testament; 1979:ix
[38] *loc. cit.*
[39] Ladd, G, 1996, *The Presence of the Future*; Eerdmans: Publishing, USA - refer to p. 10-26
[40] Ladd, 1996:25-26
[41] Buber, Martin, *Two Types of Faith*; by Syracuse University Publications in Continuing Education (first published 1951) pg 14
[42] Buksbazen, Lydia, 1955, *They Looked for a City*, Friends of Israel Gospel Ministry, NY, USA; 1955
[43] Based on William T. Arnold's article and modified and adapted by Roni Mechanic. Mr. Arnold commented with approval on my modification:
[44] Stern, David; *Jewish New Testament Commentary*, 1992:396
[45] Stern, David H.; The Complete Jewish Study Bible, 2016:1620
[46] https://www.biblestudytools.com
[47] Rothschild, 1990:26
[48] Mahatma Gandhi, From the film: *The God of Small Things*
[49] Gandhi, Mohandas K.; *An Autobiography, or My Experiments with Truth*; Penguin Books, London, UK; 2007:103
[50] ibid pgs. 103-104
[51] Mahatma Gandhi, From the film: *The god of Small Things*
[52] https://www.todayintheword.org/issues/2007/6/theology-matters/
[53] http://halleluyahscripturesreview.com/dr-chris-koster/
[54] https://en.wikipedia.org/wiki/Kyrios
[55] https://en.wikipedia.org/wiki/Ebionites
[56] Samuelson, A User's Guide to Franz Rosenzweig's Star of Redemption 1999:163
[57] https://www.svots.edu/profile/dr-albert-s-rossi
[58] https://en.wikipedia.org/wiki/Deuterocanonical_books
[59] Sunday Express: February 3rd, 1974, p 13
[60] Goldberg, Louis; *Are there Two Ways of Atonement? Confronting the Controversies;* Lederer Messianic Publications, Baltimore, USA; 1992:5
[61] Sunday Express: February 3rd, 1974, p 13
[62] https://i.pinimg.com/736x/4b/74/4e/4b744ec263f9472c39730e7769513722--muddy-waters-history-quotes.jpg
[63] Allen, Jonathan; A Profile of Jewish Believers in the UK Church (2018),
[64] https://pmpygame.com
[65] reddit.com: goldiespapa. Dec 26, 2018, 9.41 AM
[66] Rothschild, 1990:325
[67] https://www.crossway.org/jipacker/

[68] Packer, Knowing God, 1998:39-40
[69] ibid 24
[70] Rothschild, 1990:326
[71] ibid pg. 327
[72] https://en.wikiquote.org/wiki/Helena_Petrovna_Blavatsy
https://www.biographyonline.net/women/annie_besant.html
[73] Rosenzweig, Star of Redemption, 1990:328
[74] *loc. cit.*
[75] ibid pgs. 328-329
[76] ibid pg. 329
[77] *loc. cit.*
[78] https://preachersinstitute.com/2015/08/31/masoretic-text-vs-original-hebrew/
[79] https://www.britannica.com/topic/Septuagint
https://en.wikipedia.org/wiki/Septuagint
[80] Rothschild, pg. 330
[81] Hertz, Joseph H.; The Jew in South Africa, (Joseph Herman), Bibliolife, Milton Keynes, UK; 1905
[82] https://www.poemhunter.com/poem/first-they-came-for-the-jews/ p 199
[83] Rosenzweig, 2005: 331
[84] https://reslater.blogspot.co.uk/2012/01/cs-lewis-grief-observed-quotes.html
[85] The Collected Works of St John of the Cross, Translated by Kieran Kavanaugh (Translator), Otilio Rodriguez (Translator)). The Collected Works of Saint John of the Cross (includes The Ascent of Mount Carmel, The Dark Night, The Spiritual Canticle, The Living Flame of Love, Letters, and The Minor Works) Revised Edition 2010 by St. John of the Cross (Author).
[86] https://en.wikipedia.org/wiki/Kavanah#In_Chovot_HaLevavot.Chapter 31
[87] Rothschild, 1990:146
[88] https://abcnews.go.com/Politics/deepdive/obama-legacy-promise-hope-44597110 (U.S. Capitol in Washington, Jan. 20, 2009)

From modernity to post-modernity

Modern age	Post modern age
production	consumption
Community life	fragmentation (individualism)
Social class	Identity from other sources
Family	Families (many options)
A belief in continuity and situation	Breakage with the past/tradition
A role of education	Education for what?
A one-way media	Duality of media (choice/interchange)
Overt social control	Covert control (CCTV etc)
Nationhood	Global
Science aided progress and finding the truth	Science is only one source of knowledge – plurality of truths now
Structure/security/place/stability **YOU KNEW WHO YOU WERE**	**Confusion/lack of structure/ incessant choice** **YOU CREATE WHO YOU WANT TO BE**

[90] https://www.merriamwebster.com/dictionary/numinous.
[91] https://en.wikipedia.org/wiki/Pirkei_Avot;
https://www.myjewishlearning.com/article/the-amidah/
[92] Ladd, 1996:98
[93] Ladd, George, *The Presence Of The Future*, 1996:10-26)
[94] Larsson, Goran; *Bound for Freedom,*, Hendrickson,, USA; 1999:96
[95] Rothschild, 1990:340
[96] Rosenzweig, 1990:328, p 334

✡

את אֶת

ALEPH - TAV

Notes

Roni Mechanic

Printed in Great Britain
by Amazon